FROM SUN TZU TO XBOX

WAR AND VIDEO GAMES

ED HALTER

THUNDER'S MOUTH PRESS
NEW YORK

From Sun Tzu to Xbox: *War and Videogames*

Published by
Thunder's Mouth Press
An Imprint of Avalon Publishing Group, Inc.
245 West 17th Street, 11th floor
New York, NY 10011

AVALON
publishing group incorporated

Library of Congress Cataloging-in-Publication Data is available.

ISBN: 1-56025-681-8
ISBN-13: 978-1-56025-681-6

9 8 7 6 5 4 3 2 1

Book design by Maria E. Torres
Printed in the United States of America
Distributed by Publishers Group West

For Garrett Scott, who
brought clarity to chaos.

CONTENTS

INTRODUCTION
AMERICA'S ARMY GOES TO WAR

IN THE MIDDLE of May 2003, American troops invaded Los
Angeles. Major media largely overlooked this particular action,
though it was part of a wider campaign that had achieved a persistent presence in the news. Chopping through a clear blue California sky, a cluster of Black Hawk helicopters swept over
downtown, then hovered above the glass-curtained main complex
of the Los Angeles Convention Center as pedestrians glanced
upward in surprise. U.S. Special Forces, clad in green camouflage
and clutching machine guns, descended from the copters onto a
building's roof, rappelled down its wall to the ground, then
stormed the Center's entrance. Traffic halted on Pico Boulevard

as some civilians rubbernecked in disbelief, while others cautiously fled—no doubt wondering whether the troops were here to tackle an anthrax scare, dirty bomb, sleeper cell, or some other impending threat to Western culture by Those Who Hate Us. A mere two weeks after President Bush had declared the end of major combat operations in Iraq, had the war on terror found its new front, right in the heart of the global entertainment industry?

Well, yes and no.

After all, this was Los Angeles, so surely a few of the of the more steadfast lunchtime crowd were media-savvy enough to notice that seemingly unworried camera crews accompanied the soldiers, tracking their advance into the Convention Center. Or that one helicopter had chosen to position itself directly above a building that sported a large-scale fabric advertising banner, emblazoned with a photograph of a soldier's face, the Army's logo, and the slogan "Empower Yourself. Defend Freedom." Looking past the banner's left, passersby would have noted that some more gargantuan signage likewise draped the Convention Center's entrance, with a different, but no less familiar logo: the classic tripartite-swish icon of Atari.

The Army wasn't here for reasons of homeland security—at least, not directly. These Special Forces had been ordered to invade the Electronic Entertainment Expo, or E3, the burgeoning video game industry's major annual showcase and convention. Their mission was to promote the latest version of *America's Army*, a cutting-edge computer game created by U.S. military itself as a recruitment aid, which had so far met with remarkable success from players, critics, and game industry professionals. A cunningly designed first-person tactical shooter (the same genre as the globally popular online antiterrorist fantasy game *Counter-Strike*) *America's Army* had been launched about a year earlier, made available to download for free from GoArmy.com, the branch's official recruiting Web site, on July 4, 2002. Those interested in playing could also visit their local Army recruiting center, and pick up a smartly packaged game disk, or find one in a number of different gaming magazines.

Downloaded over 2.5 million times in its first two months, *America's Army* quickly became a phenomenon in gaming circles, where carpal-tunneled true-believers chattered avidly about it for weeks, causing precipitous zigzags to descend down the message forums of innumerable Internet gamer haunts. No fewer than eight gaming publications bestowed best-of-show awards upon *America's Army* following its prerelease unveiling at E3 2002. One, the popular and snarky game-culture cartoon site Penny Arcade, declared it the "Best Misappropriation of Taxpayer Dollars Ever." "More than one million gamers have the Army to thank for a killer free video game," raved nerdcasters TechTV. By 2005, the number of registered users for *America's Army* exceeded five million. Suddenly, the Army was wicked cool. And indeed, the Army spent over $7 million developing the game—so good a thing it was at the very least getting some decent PR out of it.

Like the traditional Army swag of T-shirts and bumper stickers—but much, much hipper—the game functioned as an innovative means of extending brand awareness, delivered in a highly detailed, highly addictive package. "What this means," Major Chris Chambers, Deputy Director of the Army Games Project, explained to a reporter for *The Mac Observer*, "is that we make connections with Americans who might not have had a connection with the Army. We use the video game to make that connection. We know we've got a great game but the game is also great in terms of the story it tells about the soldiers that are in the Army and why they do things the way they do." These connections included involvement in "grassroots" *America's Army* tournaments held at gaming cafés, loft LAN parties (where gamers rig their computers together to create a small local network), conventions, and other locales, where the Army might send a recruiter to hang with the gamers, complete with an Army-logoed Hummer full of recruitment-related brochures and freebies in tow.

Traditional publicity stunts at E3 involve costumed characters, celebrity-geek lectures, giveaways, and "booth babes," those female actress-models hired to staff displays for a typically estrogen-challenged crowd. In order to highlight the upcoming release of *America's Army: Operations*, then the latest update to their already famous image product, the Army staged a maneuver called a "Battlefield Casualty Evacuation" on the convention floor of E3 2003. Around a theatrical mock-up of a

Middle Eastern urban setting, a team of soldiers rappelled from the ceiling onto the convention floor, picked up a uniformed mannequin from one part of the floor, and escorted it into the entrance of the fake building. The building displayed the red, white, and blue *America's Army* logo at its top; an artful smattering of blood-colored paint on its left leg represented the dummy's injury, along with some rips in its olive jumpsuit. Soldiers barked orders to one another in the course of the maneuver. "More bad guys, let's roll it!" exhorted one as a team of six men carried the dummy off to imaginary safety, surround by the sounds of fake firefighting.

Bad guys. Today, the term has become standard soldierly slang for enemy combatants. It's no doubt linguistically useful to have one short Anglo-Saxon name to encompass the confusing range of possible antagonists in a situation as complicated as the insurgency in Iraq, the ongoing conflict in Afghanistan, and the greater war on terror. *Bad guys* could be Al Qaeda terrorists, Iraqi insurgents, urban looters, Taliban warlords, or the resisting elements of wherever else U.S. troops get dropped. Hearing it uttered in the context of E3, one can't help but speculate whether this flexible appellation's etymology springs from video games. For a generation of soldiers who came of age slaying a monstrous array of "bad guys" in *Doom*, *Tomb Raider*, *Resident Evil*, or *Halo*, such a transposition of terms from aliens to Iraqis would be natural, even subliminally comforting, in its simplicity, and puts a new spin on the concept of "demonizing" the enemy. Depending on your point of view, it's a use of language that's either part of the horrors of war, or just a means to get the job done.

America's Army itself employs the more official military lingo OPFOR (Opposing Forces) to designate enemies in the game. "OPFOR" works in much the same way as "bad guys," quickly dehumanizing human targets with a bureaucratic-scientism, though without the boyish conceit. When networked teams fight one another inside *America's Army*, an interesting thing occurs. Your opponents' team appears as OPFOR to you (slightly swarthier than U.S. troops, and sometimes mustached), but your team in turn appears to be OPFORs from your opponents' perspective. Thus players can only fight as members of the U.S. Army, or in later versions of the game, as non-American "indigenous forces." In *America's Army*, you always play on the right side.

Indeed, thanks to its Internet presence, many of those who joined up in *America's Army* weren't Americans. On one of the Frequently Asked Questions lists on the *America's Army* Web site, a hypothetical reader inquires, "I am not in the United States, can I still play the game?" The provided answer: "Yes, we have official servers in Europe as well! There are no restrictions on who can play *America's Army*. We want the whole world to know how great the U.S. Army is."

Keeping It Real

Of course, at E3 that day, there were no bad guys at all. Temporarily blurring the lines between real and imaginary, live and virtual, was what *America's Army*'s E3 stunt was all about. The Army created a fake battlefield with actual soldiers, who saved a mannequin by performing authentic maneuvers, all staged for cameras and journalists. The PR message was to convey the theme of *America's Army*'s "realism"—a concept that had become a buzzword in post-2000 game design, as much for the Army as for Microsoft, Rockstar, Electronic Arts, or any other commercial game designer or publisher. Like the most successful selling points, "realism" was a slippery term. It could refer to the increasingly cinematic qualities showcased in games for next-gen console systems like the Playstation 2 and Xbox, whose images boasted better graphics and more fluid movement than ever before available to a consumer product. It could be about how savvy and responsive the game's AI was—meaning the intelligence-simulating programming that controls a player's computerized opponents. Or it might concern all the myriad of artistic details that appeared to correlate to the sensorial clutter of nondigital existence: the background hum of traffic, garbage in the streets, or the muttered comments of AI-controlled supporting players.

For war games especially, it could refer to the veracity of any number of real-life elements: geographical environments based on real locations, accurate depictions of weapons that could only fire a certain amount of rounds before reloading, or ballistics that caused missiles to travel in arcs that replicated real-world physics. *America's Army* offered all these components, with an added hook lifted from the war in Afghanistan. At a time when images of this conflict were rare, *America's Army* offered privileged glimpses from the front lines, in the manner of old-time newsreels. Some of the backgrounds in the game were lifted from video footage of Afghan landscapes. Early in the game's history, its official site included a "Stories of Afghanistan" blog by an actual American soldier who, as the site stated after its launch in 2002, "is also capturing ideas, facts, and footage that may be used in future iterations of the *America's Army* game." All this at a time when news footage and images from Afghanistan were notably scarce in mainstream media; minds hungry for information about the war could be satisfied by virtual re-creations of reality, albeit reshaped according to the Army's PR objectives into an anonymous, vaguely central Asian theater of operations.

Stressing *America's Army's* connection to the real soldiers of the U.S. Army remained an important facet of the game. In later versions, *America's Army* offered a special online perk to real soldiers who played. If they entered in a valid military e-mail address, the players could have their online avatars wear the Army's yellow star logo, thus announcing to other players that they were actual U.S. soldiers. By early 2005, according to an Army Public Affairs Office press release, more than six thousand soldiers bore the star inside the *America's Army* world, where they could "provide actual Soldier stories to other gamers through an integrated player-chat tool."

In promotional trailers screened at E3 and distributed online, the designers of *America's Army* stressed how closely they worked with the real America's Army. Video montages showed how training grounds in the game had been closely modeled from real Army training grounds; in some shots, it is difficult to see the difference between the two. An important feature of the game is that players need to follow the Army's official Rules of Engagement. Shoot a fellow soldier, for example, and your character ends up in a tiny jail cell for a ten-minute stretch, unable to continue the game, as a woeful, mocking harmonica plays the blues in the background.

So, whether by grand intention or not, the Army was indeed fighting a strategic element of President Bush's War on Terror: the PR front, looking to win the hearts and minds of Americans. Though *America's Army* had essentially been concocted in-house by the military—graduate students and researchers at the Modeling, Virtual Environments, and Simulation (MOVES) Institute at the Naval Postgraduate School in Monterey, California, had created it from the Unreal Engine, the basic programming guts inside many major commercial game franchises, from *Tom Clancy* to *Harry Potter*—its implementation was overseen by global advertising giant Leo Burnett Worldwide of Chicago, who also creates campaigns for such well-known brands as Nintendo, Philip Morris, Kellogg's, Heinz, Disney, and McDonald's. Leo Burnett had introduced the "Army of One" campaign in 2000, and beefed up the branch's Internet presence through an enhanced recruitment Web site, online ads, and a reality-TV-style Web-based series about the one recruit's journey through boot camp. "If you're ready to stop playing games," read one of Leo Burnett's Web ads for the Army, atop an animated video game character, "we're ready for you." By 2005, the Army contracted Burnett for over $200 million a year—the largest advertising contract for any American government agency.

America's Army became part of a number of national recruitment outreach efforts, including the Army College Tour, the GameRiot gaming tent at summer music festival Lollapalooza, and the Army's Takin' It To The Streets campaign, or "TTTS." According to the Pentagon's Defense Contracting Command site, TTTS was "designed to educate and inform African-American high school, college and workforce prospects about the U.S. Army and its many career opportunities" by touring a tricked-out Hummer to schools, malls, and events. Potential African-American recruits could sample *America's Army* in the TTTS "interactive arena," or shoot hoops with an actual basketball net soldered to the back of the customized military vehicle.

The Target Shoots First

The rationale behind *America's Army* preceded 9/11, however. In 1999, the Army's recruitment figures were at a three-decade low. In response, the Pentagon increased recruitment budgets to an unprecedented $2.2 billion a year, and Congress called for "aggressive, innovative experiments" to increase enrollment.

That same year, Lieutenant Colonel E. Casey Wardynski, an economics professor at West Point, suggested to the Army's Deputy Chief of Staff for Personnel and its Deputy Assistant Secretary of the Army for Military Manpower that a video game could be an effective means to reach the new Gen-Y pool of potential soldiers. Wardynski became the head of the Army Games Project, which led to the creation of *America's Army*.

If recruitment seemed important during the economic boom time of the Clinton years, when the Army had to compete with a healthy job market, it became an even more pressing issue after the 9/11 attacks. In 2003, when the Army rolled out its latest video game to the welcoming crowds at E3, the Bush administration and political analysts still predicted a worldwide conflict with no clear end in sight, and American forces were already occupying two far-flung nations. Never before had the U.S. fought a modern conflict of this scale without a draft. But somebody had to fight the global war on terror, and connecting the Army's image to something high-tech, fun, and hip could only help. Too messageless to be called propaganda, *America's Army* was simply any client's dream of a successful marketing campaign. It succeeded with one of the primary purposes of brand marketing: get the brand name out there. With millions of players registered worldwide, *America's Army* was certainly getting its eponymous underwriter's identity to the gaming world.

Before 2002, only a minority of gamers would have much paid attention to the goings-on of the real U.S. Army—at best, they

From Sun Tzu to Xbox

might maneuver their camo-clad fantasy counterparts through the latest computer-based spy thriller. But now, with the success of *America's Army*, the real America's Army had, for a moment, become video-game industry rock stars, at a time when that industry itself had taken a quantum leap into the mainstream consciousness and entertainment business credibility.

In 2002, video and computer games raked in a record-breaking $28 billion in global sales, according to the Interactive Digital Software Association. As frequently noted in the subsequent slew of news items on the rise of the gaming industry, the Hollywood global box office earned less than $21 billion that same year. The comparison may be slightly specious—any *Entertainment Weekly* reader knows that twenty-first-century movie studios make the bulk of their income on ancillaries like television, DVDs, and merchandise, not at ticket booths of attendance-dwindling theaters—but the potent symbolism of those figures proved more compelling than the cogency of their number-crunching. Video games had leaped up a level from juvenile, nerdy subculture to cool, happenin' mass culture, thanks to new generation of console games, the continued spread of PC titles, and a growing population of both younger and older gamers. As the kids who played Atari and Nintendo during the Reagan days grew up, they kept playing the newer games; their Gen-Y younger cousins were raised with the Internet and taught with software in elementary school, so they took to games even more easily.

Playing the media was nothing new for the American military, of course. For nearly a century, the Army and other U.S. service branches had worked with the major film, television, and radio corporations on projects to help boost the military image. The first Hollywood film to win Best Picture, a sky romance called *Wings*, was made with the cooperation of the Army's Air Corps. *Top Gun*, the 1986 Tom Cruise aerial vehicle—produced with the assistance of the Navy—reportedly increased enrollment by a ridiculous 400 percent; the Navy even set up recruiter tables at movie theaters once they realized what was happening. But *America's Army* was something different: this game had been almost completely developed and produced within the military itself, not by a corporate partner. It was as if, in 1920, the Army had marched into the small but booming town of Hollywood, set up its own studio, and produced one of the top-grossing motion pictures of the year. (And by fall of 2005, *America's Army* ultimately became a commercial product itself, when French game developers Ubisoft released a for-sale console version for Playstation 2 and Xbox.)

But this online blockbuster wasn't produced to sell tickets or DVDs. Because of the Bush administration's timing, *America's Army* was working to sell the concept of signing up one's life to be a part of a very real, and deadly war, one that the American public increasingly perceived as rife with moral and political complications, and initiated on questionable presumptions. So surely there were some pangs of concern in reaction to all the nifty news coverage *America's Army* was getting—a bit of panic on the part of parents, perhaps. Weren't video games, well, bad for you? Didn't the news tell us, only months earlier, that the 9/11 terrorists used *Microsoft Flight Simulator*, a popular off-the-shelf PC game, to train for their deadly deeds? Wasn't the D.C. sniper a big fan of "one shot, one kill" video games like *Counter-Strike*? Didn't the kids who perpetrated the Columbine massacre practice countless times earlier by slaughtering ene-mies in *Doom*? For decades, parents and congressmen had wrung their hands over the ideas that video games were teaching our kids to kill. Now, the government appeared to pro-mote that same fact in the cause of national security.

A "Parents' Info" section of the *America's Army* site offers an attempt to assuage such concerns. "With the passage of time," it calmly explains, "elimination of the draft and reductions in the size of the Army have resulted in a marked decrease in the number of Americans who have served in the Army and from whom young adults can gain vicarious insights into the chal-lenges and rewards of Soldiering and national service. There-fore, the game is designed to substitute virtual experiences for vicarious insights." Long after the days of World War II and uni-versal service, the military experience was no longer a shared cultural experience for Americans, and the generations raised post-Vietnam could just as well have parents who rejected mili-tary culture wholesale, or at best ignored its existence. *America's Army* was a means to reinvade American popular culture, using a form of media that was likely to bypass parents altogether.

Special Forces at Work

America's Army came at a time when the real Army, and all the branches of the U.S. armed forces, were undergoing Transformation. "Transformation" was the buzzword for a full-scale rethinking of the entire American military: an extreme technological upgrade for the twenty-first century. Key concepts were "jointness," or the cooperation across different branches of the military, and "networking," which referred to the need to connect all forces by advanced communications and information systems. Military leaders wanted America's armed forces to become more mobile, lightweight, and flexible, able to be deployed at a moment's notice anywhere on the globe.

As a philosophical vision, transformation coincided with a new geopolitical reality. Gone was the old dyadic Cold War clash of the superpowers, in which the American military trained to anticipate such conventional hypothetical scenarios as Soviet tanks rolling into California or MiGs blitzing Boston. In an imminent future of rogue states and terrorist operatives, "asymmetrical warfare" between forces with widely different capabilities would become the norm. For this new global scenario, the military needed quick-thinking, adaptable war fighters. These wars would be fought block by block in city streets; for the most part, there would be no front lines, and electronic networks could provide the cohesive chain of command with more scattered groups of soldiers.

Quick-thinking individuals who effortlessly operated inside high-tech communications systems? Sounds like your average video game player might be a match.

After 9/11, as American culture shifted into new arrangements of patriotism, paranoia, and anxiety, the country's military and political power became central topics of debate and consternation in ways they had not been before. From live embedded reporting, to digital photography at Abu Ghraib, to Web sites displaying the caskets of American casualties, the question of how new media fit into the new world order became an important and contested element of how this war would be seen Stateside.

An October 2002 feature on *America's Army* by Salon.com columnist Wagner James Au is illustrative of this debate. Lauding *America's Army* as an important and necessary means to battle terrorism, he compares the game to Frank Capra's *Why We Fight* series of government films produced during World War II. For the war on terror—"which," Au writes, "if we parse out the diplomatic niceties, really means a war on Islamist militants, and the nations who back them (beginning with Saddam's Iraq)"—*America's Army* is "*Why We Fight* for the digital generation." Inspired by hawkish thinkers like Christopher Hitchens, Au waxes poetic on the potentials that *America's Army* embodies—how the future of American policy can merge an aggressive global military stance with the needs of homeland

security, all predicated on the country's redoubtable technological prowess. You can see them in the field, in subsequent years,"
Au writes, "dedicated young men and women, their weapons
merged into an information network that enables them to cut
out with surgical precision the cancer that threatens us all—
heat-packing humanitarians who leave the innocent unscathed,
and full of renewed hope. In their wake, democracy, literacy and
an Arab world restored to full flower, as it deserves to be, an
equal in a burgeoning global culture, defended on all fronts by
the best of the digital generation."

This paradoxical vision of "heat-packing humanitarians" is
shared by *America's Army's* marketing. In 2003, the Department
of Defense wanted to increase the number of Special Forces soldiers. Subsequently, *America's Army: Special Forces* was
released to help with this recruiting mission. A promotional
video for *America's Army: Special Forces*, made available on its
Web site and distributed to online gaming publications, verges
on being in itself a recruitment ad. Mixing real-life video footage
of Special Forces soldiers with images from the new edition of
America's Army, the spot displays a series of titles that concate-
nate into a patriotic hymn of adver-poetry, set to a booming
orchestral score. Like much marketing copy, whether designed to
sell a soft drink, an election, or a war, it is filled with emotional,
empty language, what Sinclair Lewis called "noble but slippery
abstractions." Each line holds at least two meanings: does it
refer to the real world, the game world, or maybe both?

As long as there are forces that threaten the promise of freedom
America's Army stands ready
And in the vanguard you will find
Special Forces
The Army's quiet professionals
Qualified for independent action
Experts in unconventional warfare
Help liberate the oppressed
Become one of America's Green Berets
And subdue the enemies of freedom
America's Army
Special Forces
Empower Yourself
Defend Freedom

Understanding the Game

America's Army is an utterly contemporary phenomenon: a cut-ting-edge technological artifact, resonant with the sociopolit-ical debates surrounding the War on Terror, in a form of pop culture that has just hit its tipping point. It is part of a larger process of how American military culture has been merging with entertainment, even as the geopolitical events subsequent to September 11 have reintroduced the question of American military power back into everyday conversation. And it's not alone in portraying contemporary war through a game: in the last five years, games based on real wars have become bigger than ever before.

MIT's Henry Jenkins, who had studied the effects of video

games for over a decade, has observed that video games have taken on a peculiarly resonant role in how we are thinking about war now. "The political importance of games has been demonstrated again and again as groups struggle over how—and whether—the Iraq War should be represented through games," he writes. "The military uses games to recruit and train soldiers; the antiwar movement uses games to express the futility of the current conflict; the pro-war movement uses games to express its anger against the terrorists; the news media use games to explain military strategy; and the commercial games industry wants to test the waters to see if we are going to play war games the same way other generations watched war movies."

What does it mean to see war as a video game? Like other forms of art and entertainment, video games engage us by providing fantasies about the world. In a time of real war, games based on military themes begin to take on a more serious aura. For many, creating or even playing a game that promises a realistic experience of war verges on an inconsiderate lack of respect at best, or a manipulative attempt at propaganda at worst. Indeed, the very notion that war might be played as a game can offend, regardless of political import. "The severe discrepancy in the scale of consequence makes the comparison of war and gaming nearly obscene," Elaine Scarry observes in *The Body in Pain*, "the analogy either trivializing the one or, conversely, attributing to the other a weight of motive and consequence it cannot bear." Indeed, as *America's Army* gave way to a crowd of

From Sun Tzu to Xbox

commercial video games based on real conflicts, journalistic and academic essays on what it all meant became familiar features in newspapers, journals, and online publications.

But this twenty-first-century phenomenon connects to a deeper history of how games and war have been linked since the dawn of recorded time. For Scarry also notes that "even in a relatively confined war the events are happening on a scale far beyond visual or sensory experience and thus routinely necessitate the invocation of models, maps, and analogues," and furthermore attests to "the existence of the descriptive convention, richly elaborated by strategists, historians, political philosophers, and perhaps all who have occasion to speak about war, of conceiving of two national armed forces as two colossal single combatants." Despite any squeamishness moderns may feel at the connections between war and games, links between the two concepts and practices run far back into the oldest records of civilization.

Long before video games existed, there were ancient games that simulated war, with fantasies and legends surrounding them of how these games might be used to wage real battle. In the dawn of the modern age, these fantasies became true, as a new emphasis on the logic of strategy transformed the waging of wars. In turn, the merger of technological developments with strategic and tactical needs inspired the birth of the computer. Videogames arose within the new hacker cultures surrounding the computer, when they were still heavily subsidized by military funds. Once video games became an industry of their own, they in turn fed innovations back into the world of defense. Lately, this sporadic, even accidental interplay between video games and war has been encouraged and fostered in a deliberate manner, by a new generation of visionary thinkers from the worlds of technology, entertainment, and the military.

At the same time, since 9/11, commercial game designers are churning out a new generation of realistic games based on historical wars. Now gamers can go to their local store, pick up a virtual reenactment of the Vietnam War, World War II, the Gulf War, or even something that approximates the current wars in Iraq and Afghanistan. Unsatisfied with the versions of history that these commercial games invoke, artists, hobbyists, and activists are building their own games in response, creating a new means of cultural critique via gaming.

This book is an attempt to tell this story: to show how the development of video games has at many points in its history intersected with the American military needs, including a chunk of history that is being written right now. Consider this book a history of warfare told through video games, or a history of video games told through war. In many ways it is a history of ideas and fantasies, but dreams that became real through play. It is about how video games are accidental products of war, but have in turn become ways to think about war. In many ways it is a story unique to our time, but as history shows, we have played this game before.

PART ONE
TOY SOLDIERS

WAR AND GAMES
BEFORE COMPUTERS

A board of three feet square
Becomes a battle field
Lay out the massed infantry
And let the two enemies engage

                          —Ma Rong (A.D. 76–166)

Microsoft's *Age of Empires II*, a popular and addictive strategy game released in 2001, begins with an animated intro sequence, set in a darkened castle. In it, two medieval kings sit at a table, playing chess, close to a blazing fire. One king wears robes of red; the other, green. The king in red moves forward a pawn; it is squat and lozenge-shaped, carved with gothic curlicues. As the pawn clicks onto a new square, the movie cuts to a parallel shot of a single mounted warrior galloping through a woodland clearing. In turn, the green king moves his knight, and the movie shifts to several knights in armor galloping toward a target. Though the kings' faces are cold with the Botox-animatronics typical of turn-of-the-millennium game animations, they indicate the mounting tensions of the chess match with mechanical eyebrow-lifts and pendular head-tips. When the green king captures a pawn with his knight, a party of knights clops past a group of workers building a siege weapon, severing the construction's support lines with their swords. Scenes of escalating warfare ensue, filled with the clanging of metal armaments and a valiant, blockbuster score. Soon the battlefield turns silent. The imaginary camera tracks back to reveal a meadow laden with the meticulously rendered corpses of fallen warriors.

Anyone who has played the *Age of Empires* series knows that the experience of the game is, in fact, nothing like this. As is often the case in video games, the intro sequence is a dramatic fantasy of what the game is meant to represent—or perhaps what its developers dream it could be in a near-future world of greater processing power. In the *Age of Empires* games, you assume the godlike role of the developer of a tiny kingdom, building temples, garrisons, universities, harbors, and other such structures onto a bare map. Eventually, your kingdom can raise tiny armies, depicted by minuscule figures not much

[handwritten: relationship between war + games]

larger than a typical cursor, and head off to war with other kingdoms. In contemporary gaming parlance, *Age of Empires* and its relatives—*Sid Meyer's Civilization, Command and Conquer*, and so on—are known as turn-based strategy games, the digital descendants of old strategy board games like *Risk* and *Stratego*, updated with the logic and graphics of modern simulation games like *SimCity*.

What's clever here, however, is how this little movie encapsulates the genealogy of the game it introduces. Not only is chess an apt medieval stand-in for the *Age of Empires II*, it is in fact its direct ancestor. But this lineage from chess to PC game is more complex than one might at first assume. For not only does a game like *Age of Empires* engage the theme of war; it owes its very existence to war. Through many twists and turns, a best-selling time-waster like *Age of Empires II* was made possible through centuries of interaction between the practice of war and the practice of leisure. Games made for entertainment inspired professional games made to teach and wage war; these new, deadly serious games in turn influenced novel innovations in games for pleasure.

[handwritten: Always connected]

Gametime and wartime have never been far removed. As long has humans have waged war, they have also played it; the relationship extends back to the beginnings of civilization, and no doubt before. The earliest cultural records of China, India, the Middle East, the Americas, and Europe all reveal evidence of games of skill and chance that take the form of abstracted battle—miniature metaphors for war, primitive board games composed of props made from stone or wood, clay or porcelain: the glory and horror of warfare shrunk down to toy-sized make-believe. Cultures around the world have shaped games to represent war, and in turn have used this theme of war to enhance the experience of playing games.

How far back does this evidence go? In ancient sites in Mesopotamia and Egypt, archaeologists have uncovered small sculptures of warriors that may have been used as game pieces. We can only imagine the tiny wars that might have been played with these figures; in a sense, they may have been a part of the very first military simulations. Perhaps generals who went to battle under a king or pharaoh returned to tell the tales of their exploits, using the sculptures to describe their movements, or maybe priests acted out the melees of gods and heroes, manipulating their tiny tokens like antediluvian action figures.

Such speculation may be nothing more than modern fancy. But there are many other well-documented examples of war-themed games of distant antiquity, some of which even continue to be played up to today. Though the goals and rules of each game may differ, they share a similar form. Each requires the use of a set of game pieces—typically of different colors—that represent soldiers in an army, and a game-board grid that may be thought of as a miniature battlefield. In each game, two players employ a series of prescribed movements to outdo the other player's army, whether by surrounding his or her pieces, capturing, or removing them from the board, or controlling space on the imagined war-grounds. Western chess and the Asian game of go are only two of the most widespread and influential of these games. While some of these games may have developed out of others, the idea of a war-themed strategy game has developed independently in numerous cultures at different points of history.

Old School Emulators

In the realm of video games, ancient history begins with *Pong*, not papyrus. Most histories of the form reach back no further than the 1960s, with the invention of the first systems created to play games on early graphical display monitors or television sets. Assiduously archaeological histories might mention the invention of the digital computer in the 1940s, or early nongraphical games of chess and tic-tac-toe programmed in the 1950s as logic exercises. So why begin a book on video games with a discourse on war-themed games of thousands of years ago?

Videogames have given us a new way to look at this history: these very old pursuits can be seen as the conceptual ancestors of today's digital time-killers. Board games are the earliest attempts to create play inside a simulated environment—albeit one crafted from a hardware of clay, stone, or wood, and organized by a software of traditionbound rules of play. This differs from sports, which requires the use of the whole human body within real space, or literature, which simulates a world through language but does not allow the kind of operative actions of gaming. Thus when today's gamer moves her character through some elaborately designed three-dimensional realm, at a certain level she acts out a technologically enhanced update of the Renaissance aristocrat shifting his pawns on a chess board. Obviously, much has changed. The chess player plots exclusively against a human opponent; the gamer's rival may be nothing but a piece of software. The modern experience involves cinematic graphics, an increased emphasis on immediate reaction time, real-time remote maneuvering in virtual spaces, and complex frame-stories, while chess functions almost as pure strategy. But not entirely so: we all recognize that chess is meant, on some level, to represent battle, in a highly stylized manner. Even a game as prosaic as checkers is laid out like two sets of opposing troops.

Competitive athletics developed out of the physical needs of combat (archery and javelin-throwing being two of the more obvious examples), but board games evoke a way to think about war. If sports symbolized the physical activities of foot soldiers—the skills of hand-to-hand combat and "game-time" team survival tactics—then board games mimicked the strategizing of kings and commanders, who needed to make mental pictures of war, workable schemas, plans, and abstracts. Games can be seen as representations of an ideal, of warfare stripped down to what its practitioners might believe to be its essence. Games, in short, can be seen as simulations of warfare. (In contemporary military parlance, *models* and *simulations* bear distinct meanings. To today's Pentagon, a *model* is a physical, logical, and/or mathematical representation of a system or process; a *simulation* adds to this the dimension of representing change over time. Chessmen may roughly serve as a *model* of an army, but it is the game play that is the *simulation* a battle.)

But these simulations meant different things to different societies and in different eras. Games could be tools for teaching strategy, or they could be ways to reenact a battle for study. They could be ritualized memorials to fallen comrades. In simulating the reality of battle, some legends imagined, they might even be seen as replacements for war—something heads of state might do instead of sending their people to kill one another.

"Ever since words existed for fighting and playing, men have been wont to call war a game," writes Johan Huizinga in one of the first philosophical studies of gaming, *Homo Ludens*. "The two ideas often seem to blend absolutely in the archaic mind. Indeed, all fighting that is bound by rules bears the formal characteristics of play by that very limitation. We can call it the most intense, the most energetic form of play and at the same time the most palpable and primitive." For much of human history, the conduct of war was bound by rules and customs that closely resembled sport and games, and even overlapped with them: consider the practice of courtly war in the Middle Ages, or the highly estheticized "flower battles" of the Aztecs and their neighboring states, in which it was decided beforehand which warriors would be captured by the other side.

Homo Ludens was first published in 1938, and revised in 1944; its Dutch author composed these lines with the bloodshed of World War I in mind, and perhaps, later, the brutality of Nazi aggression still fresh in his consciousness. For he also felt that the advent of modern war had tipped humanity's propensity for mass destruction into a realm beyond the ritualized strictures of play. "Until recently the 'law of nations' was generally held to constitute such a system of limitation, recognizing as it did the ideal of a community of mankind with rights and claims for all, and expressly separating the state of war—by declaring it—from peace on the one hand and criminal violence on the other. It remained for the theory of 'total war' to banish war's cultural function and extinguish the last vestige of the play-element."

French scholar Roger Callois, who followed and critiqued Huizinga, argued that play was more separate from the activities of culture as a whole, but agreed that modern warfare had transgressed beyond its gamelike origins. "If the individual remains inhibited by fear of the law or public opinion, it nonetheless seems permissible, if not meritorious, for nations to wage unlimited ruthless warfare," Callois writes in 1958. "Various restrictions on violence fall into disuse. Operations are no longer limited to frontier provinces, strongholds, and military objectives. They are no longer conducted according to a strategy that once made war itself resemble a game. War is far removed from the tournament or duel, i.e. from regulated combat in an enclosure, and now finds its fulfillment in massive destruction and the massacre of entire populations."

The paradox of this observation is that even as practice of modern warfare began to break down social and moral limits once honored, games became increasingly important to the planning behind such events. Starting with modifications of chess, games went from being aesthetic metaphors for war, or a means for mental exercise, to becoming very real and effective tools for winning battles. Cultivated by military needs and desires, the idea of the war game would develop into not just an instrument, but influence a whole way of thinking about strategy and tactics through mathematics that would eventually result the development of computers. This militarization of gaming continues up until the current era, and worms its way through the story of video games in some unexpected ways.

Classic Gaming

In the tombs at Beni-Hassan in Egypt, dating from around 2000 B.C., a mural depicts two pairs of men each seated around low tables. Each table holds similar sets of small black-and-white sculptures that suggest tiny human figures—finger-high pillars topped with head-bulbs. The seated men curl their forefingers and thumbs around the heads of pieces near them, as if readying to move them to other places on the board. To a modern viewer, they appear to be playing something like chess. Scholars today interpret the mural as depicting two different games, called *senet* and *t'au.* Though the exact rules of either game remain unknown, scholars believe *senet* to be a race game, that is, a game in which one player's men must advance upon the board to a determined destination before the other player's men can do so—in the same class as some very old games like Parcheesi, or modern inventions like *Sorry!* The second game depicted, *t'au*, is very likely an early war game; the game's name literally means "robbers" or "mercenaries." This may be the earliest known game with battle as its theme. In his marvelously titled study *A History of Board Games Other Than Chess*, scholar H. J. R. Murray argues that the positioning of the groups of pieces resemble the "armies" found in other war-themed games, corroborated by depictions of *t'au* in various mythological illustrations from *The Book of the Dead*, which show, among other things, Pharaoh Ramses III playing a game against Isis, and a lion playing a game against an antelope. The lion, Murray notes, appears to be winning.

From the fifth century B.C. onward, ancient Greeks enjoyed a battle-themed gamed called *petteia* (from the word for pebbles, or game-pieces), which had a popular variant called "*poleis*" ("cities"). The game was played with stones of black and white on a grid of squares; players determined the movement of their pieces through strategy, rather than a roll of the dice, with the goal to surround and capture the other player's men. The "cities" may have referred to either the board as a whole—the political landscape in which the *agon* took place—or to the identity of each person's team. Either would be a fitting metaphor for the age in which the armies of Sparta might battle those of Thebes, and a man's identity was deeply intertwined with that of his *polis*. Although the game appears to have been widespread, like many aspects of ancient life, only fragmentary records of its existence and societal usage remain—a few images, a handful of literary references, and a few ambiguous artifacts.

For example, a number of Attic vases depict Trojan War heroes Ajax and Achilles hunched over a small table, playing Petteia while wearing full battle armor. Some sources believe this to refer to a passage from an epic poem, now lost, in which the warriors become so absorbed in their game that they forget to join a real battle that was already under way. On some of the vases, Athena appears between them, alerting them of the raging war, but the two men continue to stare intently at the board, as fixated as a pair of slackers at an Xbox.

According to the accounts of philosophers, skill at petteia was held in high esteem. Sophocles attributes the creation of the game to the legendarily wise Palamedes, hero of the Trojan War. Plato offers that petteia, along with mathematics, geometry, and astronomy, originated in Egypt as inventions of Thoth, the Egyptian god of wisdom. In the *Republic*, he uses the development of petteia expertise as an illustration of the process of learning in general, including training for combat.

"Is it so easy that a man who is cultivating the soil will be at the same time a solider and one who is practicing cobbling or any other trade," Socrates asks, "though no man in the world could make himself a competent expert at petteia or the dice who did not practice that and nothing else from childhood but treated it as an occasional business? And are we to believe that a man who takes in hand a shield or any other instrument of war springs up on that very day a competent combatant in heavy armor or in any other form of warfare—though no other tool will make a man be an artist or athlete by his taking it in his hand, nor will it be of any service to those who have neither acquired the science of it nor sufficiently practiced themselves in its use?"

The general term for a petteia game board, *plinthion,* was also used to refer to a column or mass of troops. Elsewhere in *the Republic*, Plato evokes petteia in a discussion of a fight between two cities. In *Politics*, Aristotle states that "anyone who by his nature and not simply by ill luck has no state is either too bad or too good, either subhuman or superhuman—he is like the war-mad man condemned in Homer's words as 'having no family, no law, no home;' for he who is such by nature is mad on war: he is a non-cooperator like an isolated piece in a game of petteia." Aristotle compares the man without a city (*apolis*) to the *azux*—a term used for a piece on the game board that has been isolated, and thus left defenseless. Polybius found the game to be a convenient metaphor for warfare in his *Histories,* writing that Scipio Africanus "destroyed many men without a battle by cutting them off and blockading them, like a clever petteia-player."

When Rome imported Greek culture wholesale, petteia

arrived with it, morphing into a game Romans called *ludus latrunculum*, or *latrunculi*, the "game of mercenaries." Its game pieces were called *latrones* (mercenaries) or *milites* (soldiers). Latrunculi was popular with legionaries posted at the empire's distant edges. Boards and game pieces have been found in forts as far way as Britain, with one unearthed from Hadrian's Wall, as well as in the homes of wealthy aristocrats, who would wage miniature battles while safely ensconced in their Palantine villas and seacoast resorts. Ovid remarks that wealthier aficionados played with game pieces made of carved glass or even precious gems; perhaps they did so on the boards of fine marble and silver uncovered by archaeologists. That the denizens of this famously militant and aggressively expansive empire might revel playing the role of a little Caesar seems a completely unsurprising congruence. *Laus Pisonis*, a minor poem written in the first century A.D., includes a rather florid and dramatic description of latrunculi game play:

> *Cunningly the pieces are disposed on the open board and battles are fought with soldiery of glass, so that now White blocks Black, now Black blocks White. But every foe yields to thee, Piso; marshalled by thee, what piece ever gave way? What piece on the brink of death dealt not death to his enemy? Thousand-fold are thy battle tactics: one man in fleeing from an attack himself overpowers him, another, who has been standing on the look-out, comes up from a*

distant corner; another stoutly rushes into the melee and cheats his foe now creeping on his prey; another courts blockade on either flank and under feint of being blocked, himself blocks two men; another's objective is more ambitious, that he may quickly break through the massed phalanx, swoop into the lines and, razing the enemy's rampart, do havoc in the walled stronghold. Meantime, although the fight rages fiercely, the hostile ranks are split, yet thou thyself are victorious with serried lines unbroken or despoiled maybe of one or two men and both thy hands rattle with the prisoned throng.

Whether latrunculi could ever be this thrilling, we may never know. Games aficionados have pored over these allusive words in search of the lost rules of the latrunculi, which remain obscure, though the *Pisonis* poet strongly suggests the game involved somewhat complex military-style strategy. In fact, the winner of a game was dubbed *imperator* (general) or *rex* (king).

What's clear as well is the way in which a technology even as ancient as the board game can be used to envision battle, evoking a mental picture aided by a board and tokens. In the imagination of the *Pisonis* poet, a few tokens on a square grid provide sufficient means to conjure a cunning battle-simulation, filled with pleasurable tension and excitement, but cleanly bereft of bloodshed and sorrow. It is an early example of how war games, when created for entertainment, present an idealized drama of war.

Barbarian Inventions

Early northern European cultures enjoyed their own versions of these games. Some historians argue that the Viking *hnefatafl* (and its equally unpronounceable cousins, the Welsh *gwyddbwyll* and the Irish *fidchell*) descended from latrunculi, exported via Rome's military campaigns. Played by the Norsemen of the Dark Ages on complicated intersecting grids, hnefatafl in turn proliferated through their own raids and conquests, spreading to Iceland, Ireland, and Saxon Britain. A couple of hnefatafl-related riddles from Scandinavian sagas relate the game to a mythological vision of war, with warrior-women and great dragonlike beasts. "Who are the maids that fight weaponless around their lord, the brown ever sheltering and the fair ever attacking him?" one asks. (The answer: the game pieces in hnefatafl.) "What is that beat all girdled with iron which kills the flocks? It has eight horns but no head," poses another. (The answer is the *hnefi* or head-piece of the game.) In the Welsh epic *The Mabinogion*, the knight Peredur enters the Castle of Wonders to find a magical gwyddbwyll that moves on its own, the pieces "playing against each other, by themselves." "The side that he favored lost the game," the Mabinogion relates, "and thereupon the others set up a shout, as though they had been living men."

The tiny wars fought on the game boards of ancient Europe indeed produced nothing but fantasy. Although the lore and literature of premodern European games show that they were work on nonmilitary projects; in some cases, they were involved in the protests against the Vietnam War—the very event that was, in a sense, underwriting their way of life. Levy attests that "many of the hackers were sympathetic to the antiwar cause" at MIT and had done work on hooking up phone lines for protest centers and organizing marches. Brand speaks with a rare female hacker named Pam who left programming at Berkeley because she found the work "just too disillusioning." But she recalls that other members of her lab threw themselves into leftist antiwar activities. "During the Cambodian Invasion demonstrations in Berkeley a group of us got together and designed a retrieval program for coordinating all of the actions on campus," she tells Brand. "It was a fairly dead system, but what it did was it brought together people who had never worked together before and started them talking and thinking about how it was actually possible to do something positive with technology, when *you* define the goals."

The fact that this generation of countercultural computer bums had been produced within a military-subsidized infrastructure was not the only seeming contradiction inherent in their existence. Much of the greater anti-Establishment youth movement held an antitechnological bias, a back-to-earth neo-Luddism that perceived computers as the Establishment's tools of conformity and control. This sentiment was not far removed from a commonplace suspicion about the computerization of society that one would find in any American of the period, among the uninformed of any age group or political persuasion. In the late '60s, this conflict came to head when an antiwar march in Cambridge, Massachusetts, ended with a protest at Technology Square, the ARPA-funded center for computer research activity at MIT, and subsequently a hacker haven. Brian Harvey, an MIT computer jockey who was active in the anti-war movement, reported back to his Tech Square colleagues "what low esteem the AI lab was held by the protesters," Levy writes. "There was even some talk at antiwar meetings that some of the computers at Tech Square were used to help run the war. Harvey would try to tell them it wasn't so, but the radicals would not only disbelieve him but get angry that he'd try to feed them bullshit." When the programmers heard that the march would culminate in an action right on their floor—to demonstrate how MIT's computer science affairs were implicit in the war—the lab's administrator installed bulletproof glass, reinforced hinges, and steel-reinforced barricades, fearing that the mob might destroy the millions of dollars worth of high-tech equipment.

Though the protesters were vaguely correct—the computer science labs did indeed exist thanks to ARPA largess, and there was even a CIA office in Tech Square, hidden under the fictional auspices of "R. K. Starling Associates"—the programmers asserted a professional separation from their funding source when pressed. "There's nothing illegal about a Defense Department funding research," MIT's legendary AI pioneer Marvin Minsky told Levy. "It's certainly better than a Commerce Department or

Education Department funding research . . . because that would lead to thought control. I would much rather have the military in charge of that . . . the military people make no bones about what they want, so we're not under any subtle pressures. It's clear what's going on. The case of ARPA was unique, because they felt that what this country needed was people good in defense technology. In case we ever needed it, we'd have it."

"Spacewar serves Earthpeace," the young Brand exhorts in his *Rolling Stone* article, waxing long-hair poetic on the revolutionary potential inherent in the act of hacking, of playing around with a computer for its own sake. "So does any funky playing with computers or any computer-pursuit of your own peculiar goals . . . The hackers made *Spacewar!*, not the planners. When computers become available to everybody, the hackers take over. We are all Computer Bums, all more empowered as individuals and as co-operators." Brand expressed a vision that everyday people would all become computer programmers, freeing their dependence on computers in favor of a digitalized democracy. And indeed, many of the idealistic, antiauthoritarian hackers of the kind that Brand profiled would leave the defense sector and branch out to build a brand-new realm of consumer and business technology, giving birth to the home PC and software industries, as well as the world of arcade and home video games.

But video games wouldn't remain outside the reach of real war for very long. In fact, hackers would grant the military a whole new perspective on warfare.

PART THREE
DIGITAL DEFENSE

PLAYING FIRST-PERSON WARFARE

"Even without knowing it, you're being prepared for a new age. Many of you already understand better than my generation ever will, the possibilities of computers. In some of your homes, the computer is as available as the television set. And I recently learned something quite interesting about video games. Many young people have developed incredible hand, eye, and brain coordination in playing these games. The Air Force believes these kids will be outstanding pilots should they fly our jets. The computerized radar screen in the cockpit is not unlike the computerized video screen. Watch a 12-year-old take evasive action and score multiple hits while playing Space Invaders, and you will appreciate the skills of tomorrow's pilot. Now, don't get me wrong. I don't want the youth of this country to run home and tell their parents that the president of the United States says it's all right for them to go ahead and play video games all the time. Homework, sports, and friends still come first. What I am saying is that right now you're being prepared for tomorrow in many ways, and in ways that many of us who are older cannot fully comprehend."

—Ronald Reagan, from a speech given at
Walt Disney World's EPCOT Center, March 8, 1983

In the Zone

The most famous arcade games of the genre's golden age bear the names of their clever little characters, be they protagonists or foes: *Pac-Man, Space Invaders, Centipede, Defender.* The title of Atari's 1980 tank gunner *Battlezone*, however, is different. It describes not a character, but a field of action—a new kind of space that provided the game's novelty appeal.

Freed from the side-shuffling flatland that had heretofore defined video game design, *Battlezone* evokes a sparse three-dimensional world made from needle-thin neon-green lines. All items in view are decisively angled so as to appear to enlarge and recede as objects approach or grow distant, and the player has the ability to move not just right and left, but forward and backward as well. For the first time, the arcade screen becomes an ersatz window, as the player peers into an illusory depth created via *Battlezone*'s wire-framed graphical perspective. Like geometric diagrams made from nothing but beams of light, enemy tanks prowl through a boxy, minimalist realm that stretches all around in 360 degrees, seemingly to infinity; on the horizon, jagged peaks of pyramidal mountains loom at an eternally receding distance, punctuated by a lava-spewing volcano.

In the arcade era, game graphics could be generated in one of two ways. Most games used raster displays. Like everyday televisions, a raster display creates visual patterns by assigning color to individual pixels, which are generated thirty (or more) times a second by a horizontal scanning beam. But a few, like *Battlezone*, used vector displays. Vector displays were the descendants of the Atomic-age CRTs, modified from radar oscilloscopes for use by the SAGE Missile Defense System, and later employed to generate the first games of *Spacewar!*. Instead of scanning a succession of horizontal lines in order to cover the screen, a vector system sketched images in a more direct manner, shooting its light beam back and forth to draw dots and lines, while the rest of the screen remained black. As *Spacewar!*'s developers knew, this default background meant that vector graphics were particularly suited for creating images of objects floating in the inky vacuum of outer space, an aesthetic that continued into the seventies and eighties. The classic 2-D space shooters *Asteroids* and *Tempest* were two other well-known arcade titles that used vector displays. Though grounded, *Battlezone*'s barren landscape and pitch-dark sky still evoked an otherworldly emptiness: one of its working titles had been *Moon Tank*.

The means by which a *Battlezone* player moves through the game's bare-bones 3-D world held their own revelations. Unlike most games of the time, the player does not manipulate a little "guy" through 2-D space, puppetmasterlike, as if moving a piece on a board game; rather, the player perceives the action through the perspective of the fictional tank gunner himself: you see what the gunner would see. And since the game world extends left, right, and "in back" of you, it's possible to be shot at from outside your field of vision—from a tank attacking you from your blind spot, off-screen. This aspect makes *Battlezone* an ancestor of that now-ubiquitous video game genre, the first-person shooter—games, like *Doom* and *Quake* and all their gory offspring, that portray the action through a killer's-eye view.

Though moving-image media had existed for almost a century, the movies and television never had much success with the first-person narrative format—Bugs Bunny and George Burns's fourth-wall-violating asides to audiences notwithstanding. Only the most ardent cinephiles recall the minor 1947 film-noir *The Lady in the Lake*, which adapted a Raymond Chandler novel so that "you" were gumshoe Phillip Marlowe. Pre-*Citizen Kane*, Orson Welles was ready to shoot Joseph Conrad's *Heart of Darkness* entirely from (another) Marlow's literal point of view, but plans for the film collapsed during preproduction. Nor has television memory been kind to Hugh Hefner's 1969 *Playboy After Dark*, a swanky first-person talk show that posited the viewer as yet another partygoer at Hef's. After Hef welcomed you through the doors with a little chitchat, the camera tagged along with the smoke-jacketed publisher as he introduced you to guests like Roman Polanksi and Sharon Tate, Buffy Sainte-Marie or Don Rickles, and allowed you to sit down and listen in on their conversations. The interactive nature of video games, however, made the first-person a more exciting choice, elevating it above a mere awkward gimmick. You were not just a ghost in the narrative machine: you had the power to move through the fictional world and alter it. Your actions made you an actor in the game.

Even *Battlezone*'s cabinet and controllers were specially designed to enhance its realism. Instead of a normal TV-style screen, *Battlezone* boasted a tiny porthole that mimicked a periscope's viewfinder window: gamers had to crouch down and press their faces against it, adding to its immersive feel. Standard joysticks and buttons were replaced by a unique two-joystick system meant to mimic real tank controllers. Since its vector display was monochrome, the game's colors were provided by cellophane overlays: green for the terrain, and red for a top navigational panel that held a crudely rendered radar-style map and scoreboard.

Battlezone's success at evoking a virtual world inspired some fanciful tales. According to a spurious gamer legend of the time, if a player's tank kept moving forward for at least an hour, it would finally reach these crystalline peaks, and within them find a fabled factory that was busy at work producing all those enemy tanks. In reality, any player who chose to drive away from battle in order to explore the zone would find himself zapped by a disciplinary missile, programmed for the express purpose of discouraging such a non-income-generating activity: after all, a pacifist player could potentially explore for hours on a single quarter. Atari game developer Lyle Rains reported another rumor, gleaned from a letter written to the company from a *Battlezone* fan, "who said that a friend of his had told him that if you drove far enough you finally got to the volcano, and if you drove over the top of the volcano, you could go down into the crater. And he said that inside the crater there was a castle, and that you could go inside and explore the castle. Of course, none of this was true."

While the immersive quality of *Battlezone*, enabled by its novel first-person perspective and the player's freedom of movement in a 3-D environment, may have seemed more strikingly realistic to players in 1980, such actions took place in a milieu that held some strangely unreal qualities. *Battlezone* evokes a world of tanks without drivers, an impossibly empty, clean, clear desert of cold geometric machines bereft of round, warm human bodies. When hit by an artillery shell, enemy tanks burst into a penumbra of isometric splinters, like a shattering pane of glass. The game is a vision of war without death, a purely mechanical battle, depicting nothing but a clash of data, creating the explosions of war without corporeal destruction.

Battlezone sparked literary imaginations as well. In 1982, British author Martin Amis—then an arcade-addicted laddie of barely thirty-two—published a now-obscure tome on coin-op games entitled *Invasion of the Space Invaders*. A colorful, large format guide to conquering the top games of the time, it is written in an uncharacteristically poppy, enthusiastic tone. Amis has since all but disavowed the book (according to one account, mere mention of it in his presence summons a withering scowl), but it nevertheless stands as one of the earliest and more erudite attempts to grapple with aesthetics of computer gaming. In it Amis confesses a love for *Battlezone*, describing it as a "futuristic tank game, with real tank controls, radar, enemy and terrain etched in diagrammatic silhouette, and wonderful accuracy of distance and perspective." According to Amis, its then-unique evocation of virtual space required a new way of thinking, of orienting one's self in its imaginary world. *Battlezone*, Amis writes, is "a game of special awareness.

"Admire, first, the cute controls," he suggests. "To begin with, I thought this was gimmickry—why not just a single joystick? But the double-fisted handlebars give a crucial sense of simultaneous forward and sideways movement, and give extra drama to the backward lurch. The radar gizmo is pretty perfunctory, but the screen is a gem, combining the look of op or pop art with the feel of a genuine battlezone: limited vision, nasty surprises, panicky adjustments while the enemy tank wheels slowly round to get you in its sights." (Another game-loving Brit, Steven Poole, corrected Amis's art-historical comparisons in his well-wrought 2000 study of game aesthetics, *Trigger Happy*. "Where pop art glories in colorful flat shading and razored curves," Poole coolly counters, "*Battlezone* evinces contempt for color, for material, for substance itself. Such qualities, it murmurs seductively, are illusory anyway: The edge is everything: the frontier where one plane meets another, where turret joins body, where missile meets flank.")

According to Amis, *Battlezone* drew in a particular breed of gamer, a little different than the average *Pac-Man*-fevered teen. "It attracts a relatively middle-class and elderly audience," Amis reports. "Its patrons and admirers are intense, thin-lipped characters, whose fantasy lives are clearly of martial bent. They certainly look like officer material to me." If this account can be read as more than mere parody, it would seem to match the stereotype of the hobby war gamer as a pasty, trembling milquetoast who nonetheless harbors an inner Napoleon, unleashed only through make-believe warfare—a character type perhaps even more well known in Britain than in the U.S. "These Rommels and Pattons of the arcades," Amis continues, "they seem to know exactly what is happening, they seem to know exactly where everything is. Enemy tanks fire at them, but they have judged the angle to perfection; the shells pass them by; they retreat, they manoeuvre, they come surging in again for their hit. They dream of North Africa, of carnage at Carthage, of Thermopylae. I haven't got the stamina, or the officer qualities."

PLATO's Maze

Though frequently remembered as the progenitor of first-person shooters, *Battlezone* was not in fact the first game to use such a perspective. Racing games like Atari's 1976 *Night Driver* and Vectorbeam's 1979 *Speed Freak* had provided first-person views earlier, although neither of these allowed the player much leeway in maneuvering through their barely-there virtual environments—created through a few downward-moving dots meant to represent the merest outlines of a road in darkness. And they definitely did not involve any guns. But even earlier in that decade, two pioneering first-person games emerged independently of one another, created within the online networks used predominantly by American research and educational facilities.

A game variously called *MazeWar* (named perhaps as a take-off on *Spacewar!*), *Maze Wars*, *The Maze Game*, or just *Maze* was invented in 1973 by two student programmers interning at Ames Research center. Operated by NASA, the Center was located at Moffet Field, then a major naval air base, nestled in Silicon Valley. In *Maze Wars*, a first-person protagonist wandered through the walls of a wire-framed labyrinth, shooting (or being shot by) a cadre of robot enemies. Constructed from bare-bones graphics, *MazeWar* looks like a mouse's-eye view of a laboratory experiment. By the mid-seventies, the game had spread through the academic programming world. It became such a craze that DARPA banned *MazeWar* from its ARPAnet because more than half the monthly traffic on the Net was being eaten up by online *MazeWar* matches.

A year after geeks first started blasting their way through *MazeWar*, programmers at the University of Illinois concocted a different first-person game, created for play on the now largely forgotten PLATO Network. Initially funded by the Army, Navy, Air Force, and the National Science Foundation, PLATO was a unique network, initiated in the 1960s and distinct from ARPAnet, developed specifically for creating new possibilities in education and training. By the mid-seventies, the PLATO Network extended to over a thousand educational facilities around the U.S. The network's communications capabilities enabled the invention of a number of types of applications that wouldn't see widespread impact on the Internet until the 1980s and 1990s: in the early seventies, PLATO users were already using early versions of instant messaging, bulletin board services, and chat rooms. Former PLATO users today fondly recall its distinctive orange-screened flat-panel "gas plasma" display monitors, which allowed a level of graphical sophistication which unmatched by the Internet until well into the 1990s.

Thanks to its advanced display capabilities, PLATO also became a fertile seedbed of early online, multiplayer games. Most of these were created and distributed in an unofficial manner, as university geeks explored the potential of PLATO's innovative, graphics-friendly programming language. In the PLATO environment, the sharing of information over a wide network engendered a quickly evolving ecosystem of ground-breaking software, and a subsequent community of committed gamers, a number of whom would go on to populate the commercial industry.

While the Air Force was still blasting dots in Thailand, for example, PLATO users were playing an improved, networked version of *Spacewar!*. One of the earliest games native to PLATO was *Empire*, a team-based graphical game of intergalactic conquest, initially programmed by John Daleske and Silas Warner and based loosely on *Star Trek* (the original teams were named Federation, Kazari [or Klingon], Romulan, and Orion). Programmer Jim Bowery became inspired by *Empire* to code a 3-D version of the game in 1974, which he called *Spasim*, or *SPASIM*, in the all-caps nomenclature of early coders. The name was short for "Space Simulation," though its players ended up pronouncing it like "spasm." Created for a new kind of communications network, *Spasim* in turn visualized a new kind of online phenomenon—a phantom 3-D world, an imagined but shared reality. It can be seen as the ancestor of massively multiplayer online games of today like *Ultima Online*, *The Sims*, or *World of Warcraft*. "To see a dynamic mathematical space open up in full perspective visuals for the first time was an intoxicating experience," Bowery later recalled in his online account of *Spasim*'s genesis. "As most authors must experience when they are pos-sessed of their muse, it felt like I was simultaneously creating and discovering a new universe."

Spasim did indeed open up a new universe. Bowery argues that there is an "intellectual genealogy" running from *Spasim* to several other networked 3-D games on PLATO, which in turn would inspire some of the first well-known 3-D arcade titles. After studying the *Spasim* code, Warner modified it into *Airace*, a multiuser game that gave players a first-person view of an air-craft cockpit, through which they could view a basic landscape and the planes of other players as they raced one another. *Airace* evolved into a game called *Airflight*. According to Bowery and others, *Airflight* in turn inspired programmer Bruce Artwick to develop the 1979 game *Flight Simulator*, the first such product marketed for home computer use. After several successful ver-sions of *Flight Simulator*, it was redesigned for the first genera-tion of IBM PCs, becoming the massively popular *Microsoft Flight Simulator* series, one of the longest-running, most influ-ential, and successful game franchises of all time.

"White hat" hacker Carolyn Meinel describes the immersive, surreal experience of an early PLATO flight simulator game that was probably *Airfight*: "Cyberpilots all over the US pick out their crafts: Phantoms, MiGs, F-104s, the X-15, Sopwith Camels. Vir-tual pilots fly out of digital airports and try to shoot each other down and bomb each others' airports. While flying a Phantom, I see a chat message on the bottom of my screen. 'I'm about to shoot you down.' Oh, no, a MiG on my tail. I dive and turn hoping to get my tormentor into my sights. The screen goes black. My terminal displays the message 'You just pulled 37 Gs. You now look more like a pizza than a human being as you slowly flutter to Earth.' " In another anecdote, Meinel remembers her surprise at seeing a model of the starship *Enterprise* entering the war space, which destroyed all the other aircraft and then vanished. "PLATO has been hacked!" she recalls thinking.

PLATO also provided an incubator for *Battlezone*'s ancestor, a tank simulator called *Panther PLATO*. In 1977, programmers at the U.S. Army Armor School modified *Panther PLATO* into an obscure prototype training system for tank gunners called *Panzer PLATO*, which reportedly boasted highly accurate cannon ballistics. (It is not fully clear from the scant anecdotal records of PLATO's game roster whether *Panther PLATO* was a modification of *Panzer PLATO*, or vice versa: a detailed history of this parallel Internet remains to be written.) According to Bowery, *Panther PLATO* was the direct inspiration for *Battlezone*; he claims that Atari had PLATO accounts, and therefore its employees would have experienced *Panther PLATO* prior to the brainstorming sessions that led to *Battlezone*'s development.

Electric Youth

Martin Amis's sardonic assessment of *Battlezone*'s fan base turned out to be more spot-on than he probably realized. In 1980, representatives from the Army's Training and Doctrine

Command (or TRADOC) approached Atari, expressing interest in having the company produce a modified, more realistic version of *Battlezone* that could be used as a trainer for the Bradley Infantry Fighting Vehicle, a new tanklike armored transport and battle unit that had been introduced just that year. It was the first potential government job that Atari had been offered; after all, it was a worldwide, youth-oriented consumer brand, then operating at the peak of a cutting-edge industry, not one of the stodgy military contracting firms of the mainframe era. The olive-green uniforms of TRADOC's generals must have seemed like an unlikely match for the polo-shirt, jeans, and tennis-shoe scene of Atari's offices. At many other technology companies, a potentially lucrative defense contract would be met with enthusiasm. But at Atari, where many still held to the countercultural hacker ethic of the sixties and seventies, the prospect caused rifts between programmers and management.

Today, video games are produced on the collaborative model of Hollywood filmmaking, with numerous teams of individuals working together to create a single game. But in 1981, the situation was far more auteurist: commercial games were typically the creation of a lone programmer, or maybe a team of two or three, although the game's initial concept might have been hashed out in a larger brainstorming session. In *Battlezone*'s case, the auteur in question was hotshot designer Ed Rotberg, who was not happy about the idea of his innovative arcade hit becoming a military application. "I didn't think it was a business that we should be getting into," Rotberg later told games historian Steven L. Kent in *The Ultimate History of Video Games*. "You've got to remember what things were like in the late 1970s, and where those of us who were in the business came from—our cultural background. There were any number of jobs to be had by professional programmers in military industries or in military-related industries. Those of us who found our way to video games . . . it was sort of a counter-culture thing. We didn't want anything to do with the military. I was doing games; I didn't want to train people to kill."

Nor did Rotberg want the baggage of government protocols and regulations entangling the California-style programmers' paradise atmosphere of Atari's heyday. He recalls that his protests led to a shouting match with his division's president, in front of some of Atari's highest-level executives. Nevertheless, the company remained adamant about going through with producing a prototype for the Army. Subsequently, Rotberg insisted that if his game was going to be recoded to fit the Army's specifications, he himself would have to be the one to do it—even though the Army's timetable demanded that he complete what became known as *Army Battlezone* (sometimes remembered as *Military Battlezone* or simply the *Bradley Trainer*) in a mere three months. According to Rotberg, the Army hoped to introduce a working model of *Army Battlezone* at an upcoming international TRADOC conference, where it would be publicized by a global satellite broadcast. "Since *Battlezone* was my baby, and it was *Battlezone* that they wanted to convert, and there was a deadline to get it done, I agreed to do the prototype," Rotberg remembers. However, he stipulated that his bosses "promise that I would have nothing to do with any future plans to do anything with the military. They gave that assurance to me, and I lost three months of my life working day and night and hardly ever seeing my wife." Soon after producing *Army Battlezone*, Rotberg left Atari and formed a new company with some other Atari alumni.

Modifying the coin-op *Battlezone* into an accurate training system proved to be an extensive job, involving numerous intricate alterations to both software and hardware. "First of all, we were not modeling some fantasy tank, we were modeling an infantry fighting vehicle that had a turret that could rotate independently of the tank," Rotberg told Kent. In *Battlezone*, the tank could only shoot in one direction: forward. In order to replicate the Bradley's true range, *Army Battlezone* needed to allow the player to aim within a much larger field of action. The game's new artillery were modeled on the actual weapons the Bradley carried, down to the number of rounds available before reloading. "It had a choice of guns to use," Rotberg recalls. "Instead of a gravity-free cannon, you had ballistics to configure. You had to have identifiable targets because they wanted to train gunners to recognize the difference between friendly and enemy vehicles. So, there were a whole slew of different types of enemy vehicles and friendly vehicles that had to be drawn and modeled. Then we

had to model the physics of the different kinds of weapons."
The opposing forces' tanks were designed to reflect the characteristics of Soviet-made tanks of the time. In the original game,
flying saucers occasionally buzzed into the frame and could be
shot down. These were replaced with Soviet helicopters. Also
added were U.S. and NATO tanks; prospective gunners had to
learn to tell the difference between allies and enemies, avoiding
friendly fire.

Army Battlezone also departed from the two-joystick console
of the original. Replacing the arcade controllers, Rotberg and
his team installed a strange H-shaped "yolk" controller that
looked like a stripped-down steering wheel, modeled to replicate
the actual controls of a Bradley in miniature, as well as a series
of switches and buttons to control range, choose weapons systems, and other functions—a far more complicated arrangement
that anything found at the local pizza parlor. Though the
gaming public would never have a chance to shoot down the
Soviet menace in *Army Battlezone*, its unique controller did
make its way out into the market. During Rotberg's final days,
he worked on another first-person-perspective vector game, ten-
tatively named *Warp Speed*, but left before completing it. Just
around then, Atari finalized a deal to produce branded games
with Lucasfilm, and so *Warp Speed* was finished as the 1983
arcade game *Star Wars*, using the *Army Battlezone* yolk controller. Little did young *Star Wars* fans know that as they zapped
away at wire-framed TIE Fighters zooming past the Death Star,

their hands were wrapped around a carefully constructed replica of a Bradley Infantry Vehicle's steering wheel.

What happened with the actual working models of *Army Battlezone*, however, remains something of a mystery; it appears Atari produced no more than a couple of prototypes, and there is no indication that the system was ever used for real training purposes. For decades, the fate of these few consoles remained legendary within the tiny world of arcade game collectors; despite the testimonies of Rotberg and others, some game buffs weren't convinced that the prototypes had ever been built, or had they been, speculated that they had been quickly dismantled.

One *Army Battlezone* console may have perhaps been in use as late as 1983, when a reporter from the *Christian Science Monitor* attended a conference for the Association of the U.S. Army in Washington, D.C., which included what the paper called an "arms bazaar" of over two hundred booths showcasing the latest wares of major defense contractors. "Nearby, a young civilian executive concentrated fiercely on Atari's *Battlezone* video game set up by one arms merchant," wrote the reporter, who was harshly critical of this convocation of Cold War capitalists; the youthful exec at the video game seemed to sum up his sentiments. "Somehow, as one surveyed this essence of national security at its most commercial," the reporter continued, "the words of Herman Melville came to mind: 'All wars are boyish, and are fought by boys.'"

However, in 2002, an arcade video game collector named

Scott Evans obtained one of the original *Army Battlezone* sets, and posted images of it on his Web site, Atari Games Museum (atarigames.com). According to the photos, it looks like a typical *Battlezone* console, complete with porthole-style viewer and colorful cabinet side-art depicting orange, purple, and blue stars streaking upward against a cartoon tank. A forward-facing panel of buttons, switches, and the Bradley yolk, however, had replaced its joystick shelf. Above the screen, its marquee title sign had been altered: where it usually reads BATTLEZONE, the horizontal display instead says BRADLEY TRAINER, in military-style block lettering above the cartoon of a shooting tank. An anonymous ex-employee of Atari e-mailed Evans about his find. "I am really curious where you got it," he writes. "As far as anyone knows (or is willing to admit) there were only two made. One went to a conference at Ft. Eustice [the Virginia site of TRADOC's Training Support Center] and was never seen again. The other is in my old boss's barn."

Pushbutton Warfare

By the early 1980s, video games had been around for over a decade, and had never strayed too far from the world of defense technologists. What, then, did the Army hope to achieve from *Army Battlezone*? According to Rotberg, its addictive game play was a major factor: valuable training could be embedded into a pleasant pastime that might actually encourage soldiers to hone their skills on their own. "The idea was that such a simulator could be made into a game that would encourage the soldiers to use it," Rotberg told an interviewer in the mid-nineties. "They would learn not only the basic operation of the IFV [Infantry Fighting Vehicle] technology, but would also learn to distinguish between the friendly and enemy vehicle silhouettes."

"The idea is to take an existing game system or 'device,'–I don't like the word 'game'–modify it as a modern weapons system and build necessary skills into the device," TRADOC project manager Capt. Steven J. Cox told the *Philadelphia Inquirer* in 1982. "If the trainee fires just as well on the real tank as he did on the device, then we've acquired a device that produces the same result as training on the tank for considerably less cost," a device that could successfully "test psychomotor skills" before the student had even stepped inside a real tank.

General Donn A. Starry, TRADOC's commanding general in the early eighties, oversaw the Atari collaboration. A general who led combat operations in Vietnam and Korea, Starry headed TRADOC from 1977 to 1981, and in later years helped draft the plans for Operation Desert Storm. While at TRADOC, he perceived a need for new methods of training that were more in step with experiences of soldiers who had grown up in an electronic age. "They've learned to learn in a different world," he stated in a lecture at TRADOC's 1981 commander's conference, "a world of television, electronic toys and games, computers and a host of other electronic devices. They belong to a TV and technology generation. In an era that has seen such fantastic technological achievements, how is it that our soldiers are still sitting in class-rooms, still listening to lectures, still depending on books and other paper reading materials, when possibly new and better means for training have been available for many years?" (In addition, Starry may have seen at least some of this electronic generation learning from computers via ARPAnet and the PLATO Network, both of which could be found at military educational facilities at the time.)

If Starry's ideas sound more like Marshall McLuhan than Douglas MacArthur, then keep in mind a speculation made by the former thinker. The Canadian critic argued in *Understanding Media: The Extensions of Man* that while gunpowder had been known about for centuries, the notion that the substance could be used to propel a missile through space toward a target only came about once artists had mastered linear perspective in painting. McLuhan's claim is in fact historically false—firearms existed at least a century before the early 1500s, when Filippo Brunelleschi rediscovered the lost classical system of creating the illusion of depth through compositional lines that converge in a vanishing point—but his larger message remains relevant. For although the *Army Battlezone* project would never see full fruition, the virtual 3-D space opened up by Rotberg's *Battlezone* sparked a few military minds at TRADOC to imagine a new kind of learning for battle. As in McLuhan's technofable, an artful representation influenced the art of real war.

Some game histories have speculated that the Army intended to get around normal procural protocols by purchasing *Army Battlezone* units from Atari not officially as training systems, but as just another time-killing distraction for Army commissaries, thus sneaking a bit of valuable education into the soldiers' recreation time. While this rumor remains unverifiable, a profile of early eighties training systems in the magazine *Army* mentions that "the Army plans both formal and informal use of specially programmed arcade-type games," further reporting that the Army's Armor School at Fort Knox, Kentucky, "plans to furnish day rooms and other off-duty gathering spots on the post with arcade games based on M60 and M1 tank trainers to provide amusements that will have practical value and stimulate competition in basic gunnery and command skills."

For Starry, *Army Battlezone* might have also pointed the way to the future of Army recruiting. After all, if operating a tank were really so much like playing a video game, then the malls of America were filled with prospective enlistees. "All of the people in those arcades are volunteers," said Starry. "In fact, they are paying for the use of the machines, and two-thirds of these games are military in nature—aircraft versus air defense, tank against antitank and so forth."

Starry's estimation of how many arcade games circa 1981 were military-themed is a bit high—players at that time were more likely to be jamming through the fantasy worlds of *Centipede*, *Frogger*, or *Donkey Kong*. Nevertheless, there were

indeed a significant number of titles that enacted military scenarios, even if they were typically packaged within a science-fic-
tional context. Researchers at TRADOC's Training Support
Center in Eustis, Virginia, thought that more than a few of these
had a potential for real defense training applications. In 1981,
TRADOC told *Army* that they had conducted a wide-ranging
study of the arcade game scene and concluded, "many of the
popular arcade games already have features that would be
useful for training purposes."

According to TRADOC, many of the same games that had been
designed for the primary purpose of extracting quarters from
teenagers' pockets held within them an unrealized potential for
educating future generations of American soldiers. *Red Baron*,
for example, was another first-person vector game that had been
developed by Atari programmers, designed to run on *Battlezone*'s hardware. According to *Army*'s report, this game, which
placed the player in the cockpit of a WWI dog-fighting biwing
plane, might have "something for helicopter gunners," while
Atari's legendary *Missile Command* "has controls very similar to
the Army's forward-area alerting radar (FAAR), the warning set
for low-altitude air-defense systems." Another game that the
article refers to as *Ambush* might "be used to teach junior non-
commissioned officers squad tactics." (The writer may be refer-
ring to either the arcade game *M-79 Ambush* or the home console
game *Armor Ambush*, both 2-D, third-person tank shooters.)

Imagine the strangeness of the scenario: TRADOC's generals

trolling through the local arcades, clipboards in hand, peering over the shoulders of teenagers in order to observe the finer points of the latest joystick shoot-'em-up. But would that really have been so unusual? As video game history shows, the direct ancestors of these bleeping eighties playthings had emerged from a mainframed world whose existence directly depended on America's Cold War military needs. Even if games had been invented as a side effect of military research, it took barely a decade for them to end up back at the home base, so to speak. *Army Battlezone* was only one instance of this interplay between the zones of fun and war; as a pilot program, it presaged many ideas about integrating video games into soldier training that would take hold in the 1990s with newer, more flexible technologies.

Quarter Masters

General Starry's offhand depiction of arcade games as overwhelmingly war-themed may have been debatable, but was, in fact, in line with a growing popular sentiment—among concerned parents, at least—that the games were unnecessarily violent, even militaristic. As video games became fixtures in living rooms around the world, and children absconded to local arcades with rolls of quarters in hand, the first wave of now-familiar anti-video game backlash emerged. Frequent newspaper editorials of the time express such fears from parents' groups, and in 1985, media scholar Terri Toles ventured into a local arcade to see for herself. Though probably situated to Starry's political left, Toles nevertheless shares the general's outlook in her report "Video Games and Military Ideology."

"The connection is apparent to observers who merely walk into an arcade," Toles writes. "Glancing at the names of the games—names like *Missile Command, Battlezone* and *Space War*—and the drawings of swooping fighter planes, imposing tanks and colorful explosions painted on the machines seem to prove the point. When the observer turns to see who challenges 'Is there no warrior mightier than I?' in cultured tones only to discover that the voice emanates from a machine, her suspicions are confirmed. It's not even necessary to be near an arcade to uncover the trend. Merely reading newspaper articles about video games introduces one to the worlds of 'electronic sadism,' 'martial space arts,' and 'space soldiers' that populate the arcades."

Though perhaps not as flashy as their futuristic fantasy counterparts, real soldiers were to be found at some of these game parlors. Military recruiters began visiting arcades in search of fresh enlistees; a handful of newspaper articles from the time testify that Army, Navy, and Marine recruiters all claimed to target video game players, either as official policy or otherwise. A 1982 article from the *Philadelphia Inquirer* introduces us to one Marine recruiter who frequented the teen hangouts of Woodbury, New Jersey.

Like a hunter stalking deer in a thicket of woods, John

Fisher entered the pinball arcade at the Deptford Mall. His spit-shined black shoes were as quiet as cats' paws as he weaved his way through a maze of video warriors, their lightning-fast teenage fingers zapping hordes of space invaders and homicidal robots with pulsating laser beams. Dressed in neatly pressed, buff-colored khakis, Fisher watched the action in silence, while the youngsters tested their reflexes. When there was a lull in the action, or when a youth ran out of quarters, he would move with the grace and swiftness of a matador. With an engaging smile and an open right hand, Fisher would introduce himself: "Hi. I'm US Marine Sgt. David Fisher. If you have a few minutes, I'd like to tell you some of the things the Marine Corps can offer a young man like yourself."

Another article from the same paper profiled Chief Petty Officer Julia Reed, the Navy's 1981 recruiter of the year, who was based in California. "When they play those games, they are thinking of defense and challenge," Reed claimed. "It's really no different than war. I hate to put it that way, but it's true. . . . A lot of these kids are technologically oriented, and a lot of them join up because they know the way of the world now is not a master's degree but solid training in data processing."

"I get to the arcade about 4 in the afternoon, warm up and watch them play," Reed told the reporter. "Then, maybe I'll play a game with them, and buy 'em a Coke. If I'm winning the sales job, I don't win at the game. If they're being a jerk and I can win, I try to overcome them. When we talk, I try to do 'blueprinting': find out what they are doing, what they'd like to do . . . then ask them about the Navy and whether they've ever thought about sonar or radar. Sixty percent of them will take a test. Overall, they scored a lot higher than others."

In interviews, the recruiters cited the parallels between playing video games and operating weapons systems as prime reasons to target joystick warriors. "The multi-directional locater ball on the *Missile Command* game is pretty close to the system I use for air defense," an anonymous Navy weapons specialist told the same reporter. "You have enemy aircraft defined on the screen by radar. You have your sight as an electronic cursor directed by the ball. You push a button, the missiles fire, and 'poof' no more aircraft."

Vincent Mosco's *Pushbutton Fantasies,* a 1982 academic study of the social impact of emerging video technologies, offered an account of arcade recruitment from a young gamer's perspective. The statement is attributed to one of Mosco's own undergraduate students, who was evidently a bit of an arcade whiz.

Last year I worked in a pinball arcade. As an attendant I had access to all the free pinball, in my case video games, I could play. Soon, with my combined previous skills and added accelerated skills, I have become an expert player. As a result, I have been approached on at least two separate occasions by military personnel giving me serious pitches to join the Armed Forces. My best offer came from a Major General while I was on vacation in Florida. He was so astounded by my play on the [sic] Missile Command that he offered to personally see that I would by-pass all the time-consuming preliminaries, such as boot camp, and insignificant, low-paying assignments, and start at a highly-skilled, high-paying job in ballistics. I was skeptical so I questioned his presence in the arcade, but he produced proper identification and explained that he regularly brought his grandchildren to play.

The dream of joystick jockeys becoming real warriors bubbled up into pop culture. No less an authority on 1980s adolescent entertainment than Steven Spielberg deployed this notion in his preface to Amis's *Invasion of the Space Invaders.* "The aliens have landed, and the world will never be the same again," the mogul-auteur writes. "You've got to believe it—there's a war on, and the strange thing about *this* war is if you should once make the mistake of volunteering, you'll find active service hopelessly habit-forming."

This fantasy of a secret, permeable membrane between war-themed video games and real war can also be seen in the 1983 thriller *WarGames,* in which a nerdy-cool young hacker taps into the Pentagon's missile command system via his home PC; thinking he has merely uncovered a mother lode of cool military-themed games, he starts playing one called "Global Thermonuclear War" and thereby unwittingly initiates a simulated attack, nearly triggering World War III.

A kiddie sci-fi movie from 1985, *The Last Starfighter*, bears a related premise. Alex, a young arcade hotshot who lives in a California trailer park, is visited by an emissary from another planet, who abducts him to help an alien race battle their enemies in deep space. Turns out that the teen's favorite game was actually placed on Earth to train potential star fighter pilots; the aliens had been tipped off to Alex's skills by monitoring his high scores. Soon Alex finds himself zapping a very real collection of space invaders. Though it boasted some of the earliest uses of CGI in its battle sequences, *The Last Starfighter* remains a hokey *Star Wars* derivative, hitching its fortune on the video game gimmick; but like some of the more famous teen comedies of the era, it poses Alex's challenge as an opportunity for self-realization. In ads for *The Last Starfighter*, Alex appears on the side of an empty highway at night, the road disappearing on the horizon behind him. "He didn't find his dreams," the film's tagline reads. "His dreams found him."

Graphic War

TRACOC's souped-up Atari shooter has survived in gamer lore as an oddity; many remember it as a dead-end project whose legacy, at best, involves serving as an unwitting ancestor to contemporary military video games like *America's Army*. But in fact, the story of the *Battlezone* Bradley trainer is hardly singular. Ed Rotberg's hesitations notwithstanding, the video game industry from its very beginnings had never been fully discrete from the activities of military-sponsored computer research. And even if *Army Battlezone* never saw full fruition, it existed as part of a larger post-Vietnam shift within the U.S. military that emphasized a greater investment in peacetime training, especially via simulation. The confluence of these tendencies would reach new levels of activity in the 1990s, as technological and commercial advancements in computing brought the U.S. and the world into the throes of what publicists trumpeted as the digital revolution. What had been sporadic, even chance interactions between military research and popular videogaming would strengthen substantially in a conscious effort to bring these two very different realms together for mutual benefit.

For many years generals had used games as tools for strategy, leadership skills building, and the analysis of past battles; but large-scale games could also be useful for training troops. As their ancestors had done with the tiny blue and red armies of kriegspeil, generals divided up their own soldiers into similarly named teams, set them into some artificial environment, and had them engage in mock battle, as if ordered into elaborate matches of human chess. In the early years of World War II, for example, a soldier in training before shipping off to Europe may have felt slightly ridiculous when he found himself brandishing a wooden gun and storming a supply truck that had been cheaply costumed with a canvas-and-frame to resemble a German tank. For most of the history of warfare, however, these kinds of educational theatrics were relatively rare. Until the late nineteenth century, conventional military wisdom held that the only real classroom for a soldier was the live battlefield. The graduates of this deadly academy would be graded as much by fate as prowess; war was the ultimate immersive learning experience.

But in the early years of the twentieth century, a new idea began to emerge, better suited for the age of mechanized warfare. It was the notion that a lone soldier might learn by interfacing with a solo game or personalized electronic contrivance rather than a set of other soldiers; for the first time, a combatant's relationship to his machine might prove as crucial as his relationship to his fellow soldiers. The advent of the airplane—whose speedy militarization became widely known via the celebrated World War I dogfights of Eddie Rickenbacker and the Red Baron—brought with it a unique training problem: how could aerial pilots be taught quickly and efficiently without risking their lives? In 1934, for example, almost a dozen Army Air Corps pilots perished in crashes during a single week of training. The reason: the Air Corps (the ancestor of the modern Air Force) taught its pilots to fly by watching the ground, and that particular week had brought a bout of cloudy, vision-limiting weather. In response, the Air Corps contracted Edwin Link, an aeronautics aficionado and inventor, who had constructed a novel means of teaching pilots how to fly not by orienting themselves to the ground, but instead by learning to interface intuitively with the airplane's control panels.

The son of a piano and organ manufacturer, Edwin Link grew up during aviation's pioneering days. Passionate about flight but unable to afford full flying lessons, the young Link practiced with a friend's airplane by taxiing it on the runway, trying to get a feel for its controls with his hands and feet until the system became second nature. Like other types of hacking, it was an activity that must have seemed obsessive, if not slightly pathetic, to outside observers. But it was during these faux forays that Link came upon the idea for a device called the "aviation trainer," which he soon constructed. Made of blue-painted wood, the aviation trainer looked like a miniature hobbyhorse airplane with a wingspan of twelve feet, mounted on a short, squat pedestal. The prospective pilot sat in its almost full-sized cockpit, which held a complete and realistic set of controls.

When operated like a real airplane, the "blue box" trainer's internal system of electrically powered vacuum pumps and bellows—jerry-rigged out of the guts of musical instruments from his father's Link Piano and Organ Company—moved the device around to simulate an airplane's pitch and roll. It was not essentially new—simpler models had been used as early as World War I—but it was the first to take into account the rapidly increasingly complexity of the modern airplane's controls, and the first to teach prospective pilots the skills to "fly blind," or operate the plane primarily through interacting and responding to the airplane itself, rather than orienting one's self with the land and sky. In a crude but effective manner, the Link trainer was also the first step toward training through a virtual environment.

Link's device caught on slowly. In the early 1930s, he operated a successful Link Flying School in upstate New York, but after the Depression depleted his business, the blue box found a new role as a mere midway attraction at Coney Island's amusement park. It wouldn't remain a kiddie ride for long. Following the Air Corps' training disaster of 1934–and a virtuoso stunt by Link, who flew to meet them without incident through what seemed to be an impossibly blinding storm, according to his company's official history– the Army ordered six of Link's trainers for $3,500 apiece. Other requisitions soon followed, from both commercial and military sources. During World War II, Link Aviation Devices Inc. supplied blue boxes to every aviation facility operated by U.S. and Allied forces. Link's company reportedly produced over 10,000 trainers during the war years, pumping out one blue box every 45 seconds. Today, Link Simulation & Training exists as a division of L3 Communications, a major aerospace, surveillance, and communications contractor to the Pentagon, Department of Homeland Security, national intelligence agencies, and other entities.

After World War II and the birth of the modern computer, what would become known as "simulation training" would serve a growing role in American military culture, and consequently became an increasingly lucrative business for high-tech contracting firms. Certain elements of the wartime economy became persistent business during the Cold War; as the emphasis switched from the engagement in active warfare to the cultivation of potential power—both through the arms race and the maintenance of gigantic, combat-ready standing armies—training took on a new prominence, especially since a dizzying array of new weapons systems required rapid reeducation, even if few of these nifty killing machines would never see battle.

The push to computerize simulation training came quickly. While World War II raged on, the Navy approached MIT about using computers to build a more adaptable version of the Link trainer. The idea became Project Whirlwind, and its goal was to create a computerized control panel screen that responded instantaneously to the pilot's input. Unlike the Link trainer, the Whirlwind trainer would be able to be reprogrammed to adapt to any number of different airplane configurations. But once MIT's researchers got deep into the project, the Whirlwind computer they created evolved far beyond its original purpose as a flight simulator. In the process, MIT's engineers ended up inventing most of the components of digital technology—including the display screen, the light gun, networking, the transmission of data over phone lines, magnetic core memory, and numerous other components—and the project soon morphed into an even more ambitious attempt to create a global missile-defense system, code-named SAGE. The first real-time digital flight simulator would not be realized until the 1960s, with the advent of the Link Mark I computer, designed for this purpose.

In the subsequent decades, computerized training simulations proliferated through all ranks and branches of the military. The earliest, like flight simulators, were best suited to
train for the operation of tanks and submarines—systems that
already included a mediated interface with the outside world
in their actual functioning. But as audiovisual technologies
developed, a growing multitude of electronic devices were
introduced for military training purposes, educating soldiers
in everything from firing missiles to wiring electrical panels:
the interactive, high-tech descendants of WWII instructional
films. Videogame pioneer Ralph Baer, for example, developed
a groundbreaking series of interactive video systems at
Sanders Associates that used interactive videotape and, later,
videodisc, to train soldier rifle marksmanship, antitank
artillery, and even automotive repair, all employing a regular
commercial television set as monitor.

Until the 1980s, these simulators were almost exclusively
stand-alone systems, created to teach specific tasks and specific
systems. And they were expensive. In the late 1970s, a single cutting-edge flight simulator could cost as much as $35 million,
and a tank simulator $18 million. In some cases, simulators
could cost more than twice as much as weapons systems they
were simulating. As a result of this research, the Department of
Defense was the largest underwriter of the development of computer graphics technologies until the 1990s.

Consensual Hallucination

The descendants of the Link trainers—up to and including the *Army Battlezone* project—had a significant shortcoming: Hollywood conventions notwithstanding, wars aren't fought by lone tank gunners or pilots flying solo. They're won by armies—groups of individuals working together in a complex network of protocols and decision-making. While early simulators might have helped strengthen the man-machine interface, they didn't do much in the way of teaching the crucial man-to-man interface of real combat. Sure, group interactions might have been relatively easy to teach in the days of foot soldiers, but in an age of mechanized infantry and air assaults, doing so became nearly impossible; the only adequate means of training seemed to be actual warfare.

In 1983, Major Jack Thorpe began thinking about how to create a simulator that allowed individual trainees to work together inside a shared virtual environment. Thorpe had proposed a similar idea back in 1978, when he was developing flight simulator technology with the Air Force. At the time, such a system seemed prohibitively expensive, and would probably have required an impossible amount of computing power for the necessary graphic generation. But now Thorpe was working at DARPA, and the quickly growing ARPAnet seemed to hold a solution. Why couldn't it be built as a *distributed network*, like ARPAnet then, or the Internet today? In this model, the intensive data processing would take place at each users' end, in individual consoles that would produce an image of that trainee's "perspective" within a common imaginary space, rather than emanating from a single massive central computer. Thorpe called the project SIMNET, for simulation network.

Working models were hashed out in the 1980s, and SIMNET became fully operational in 1990. DARPA supplied 238 network simulator units to the Army. By then, SIMNET could handle hundreds of individual users at once, all operating in a real-time share environment, each representing any number of different vehicle types. "William Gibson didn't invent cyberspace," *Wired* magazine wrote in 1997, "Air Force Captain Jack Thorpe did."

The Army put SIMNET to use as the Close Combat Tactical Trainer (CCTT). From the outside, the CCTT resembles a series of large grayish-green fiberglass boxes, as featureless as sensory deprivation chambers. Inside, each is an elaborate life-size mock-up of the interior of a fighting vehicle—an Abrams tank, maybe a Bradley or even a Humvee—whose "windows" are screens looking on to the SIMNET world. Adding to the claustrophobia of the unit's tiny interior is a series of sound effects to enhance the realism of the training: the faked noises of engines, guns, tank treads, or turrets rotating. The total experience can be intense enough to engender "simulation sickness" in newbies—a nauseating variant of sea- or airsickness, caused when the brain becomes confused over what's really happening versus what's being simulated.

Some sources have suggested that SIMNET was influenced by

the *Army Battlezone* project, even though the date of Thorpe's original Air Force proposal predates this. Whether *PLATO Panzer* or the networked games of the PLATO network in general inspired Thorpe is unknown. Undoubtedly, the concept of a shared virtual world was one that emerged in multiple ways in the 1970s and 80s. William Gibson's *Neuromancer* imagined a sustained, 3-D world in 1985 (famously written on a manual typewriter) and, as *Wired* notes, introduced the word *cyberspace* into the lexicon.

But another science-fiction novel of the 1980s became even more influential to the military's simulation visionaries, many of whom today cite it as an important inspiration. Orson Scott Card's 1985 *Ender's Game* posits a future Earth endangered by invasion by an insectoid alien race, the Buggers. In order to develop a strong class of warriors, the government sends its best and brightest children into space for battle training, which takes the form of video games, both two-dimensional and holographic, as well as laser-tag style low-gravity faux-death matches. The protagonist, Ender, proves to be a minimaster at these games, and rises ever higher within the ranks of this complex academy, taking on increasingly elaborate simulations and tougher training regimens as he ascends. Eventually, after an enormously trying computer-generated battle, Ender discovers the secret of the system in which he has flourished. The most recent games were not simulations at all: he was in remote control of real battalions of warships. Without realizing it, he had destroyed the entire race of Buggers and saved the earth.

Doom Generation

Back in the world of commercial video games, things had been changing, too. The rapid rise of personal computing and the development of CD-ROM storage brought PC games to a new level of popularity and design sophistication. Of course, games had always been an element of personal computing from its earliest days in the 1970s, when primitive versions of chess and *Minesweeper* were imported from ARPAnet and PLATO. But now a slew of more advanced titles were developed specifically for use on desktops and laptops. With PC games, the first-person shooter came home.

The genre's groundbreaker was *Wolfenstein 3D*, a 1994 military fantasy that popularized the first-person shooter, thereby providing a structure for video games that continues to dominate today and has pushed the form ever closer to the visual complexities of cinema. The *Wolfenstein* franchise was not new; the first in the series, a 2-D adventure game called *Castle Wolfenstein*, had been released in 1981 for the Apple II, and was written by Silas Warner, who had created key games on the PLATO network, and was followed up in 1984 by *Beyond Castle Wolfenstein*. Though popular in their day, these fairly simplistic affairs couldn't touch the impact of their 1994 grandchild, *Wolfenstein 3D,* created by id Software.

Like *Battlezone* a decade earlier, *Wolfenstein 3D* gives the player the same perspective as the game's protagonist. In this case, though, the hero is not an anonymous tank gunner, but

American World War II seargeant William "B. J." Blazkowicz, who must escape from the eponymous Nazi-infested stronghold, whose structure resembles a better-rendered the high-walled labyrinths of *Mazewar.* Several *Wolfenstein 3D* innovations have become conventions of first-person shooters today: the placement of the protagonist's gun or weapon in the bottom center of the frame; the use of the "heads-up display," a kind of console panel set apart from the 3-D virtual world of the game, indicating life force, score, and other data (a concept, not incidentally, borrowed from flight and tank simulators); the inclusion of "medical kits" that can be picked up to renew Blazkowicz's life; and the progression of increasingly powerful opponents on new levels, each culminating with a particularly tough "boss" (on the final level, Adolf Hitler himself).

In keeping with the graphics capabilities of 1994, the Nazis of *Wolfenstein 3D* are literally cartoon baddies, 2-D figures in a simple 3-D architecture, with the short, chunky bodies and large heads of anime characters. There is something both creepy and funny about seeing the perpetrators of the Holocaust reduced to icons of near-cuteness: the walls of the castle are decorated with pokey bitmapped paintings of swastikas and eagles; attacking German shepherds seem almost cuddly; and Hitler appears outfitted with a comic-book-worthy robotic attack suit. (Fanciful or no, the use of Nazi symbols and the real Nazi Party's anthemic *Horst Wessel Leid* as theme music resulted in the German government banning the game within its borders.)

Though popular, *Wolfenstein 3D* only paved the way for id's watershed 1993 title *Doom*, which brought the first-person shooter to a new level of complexity and popularity. In *Doom*, the player takes the role of a lone "Space Marine" exploring human outposts on Mars after they have been taken over by demonic alien creatures. The earliest versions of *Doom* may seem graphically crude today, but they were revolutionary advancements over their predecessors. The architecture of the Mars outpost is rendered through better texture mapping, and the first-person perspective moves fluidly through its environment (even if opponents sometimes appear as 2-D figures, like trompe l'oeil cardboard cutouts). More powerful than this graphic sophistication is the player's ability to freely explore the spaces inside the game. Finish killing off the hissing demons and flying skulls, and your Space Marine can simply poke around the dungeons, trudge through underground rivers, and look around for previously unseen elements. In fact, "secret areas" hidden in each level encourage the player to do so. In this sense, the world of Doom allows for nearly as much freedom to explore as *Grand Theft Auto* or *Halo* today.

Mod World

Another innovative aspect of *Doom* was that it was released via an internet-savvy approach, long before such techniques became the norm. Samples of the game were posted online for free; once players got a taste, they could purchase the full version to access all of the game's levels. As new versions of *Doom* were created, id distributed the original version of *Doom* free online, and made the unprecedented move of releasing its source code for free, allowing players to tinker with the game as they saw fit. At the encouragement of *Doom's* publishers, players soon took advantage of the game's modifiable nature.

Within a couple of years, there were thousands of WAD files (so called for their unique ".wad" file extensions), many of which remain available today online. While most were simply added homemade, harder levels, some went farther to cus-tomize the look and content of the game, its architecture and characters. The cultural references embalmed in these home-made environments remain frozen in mid-nineties pop culture. You can download and play a *Batman*-themed *Doom*, or, of course, a *Star Trek*- or *Star Wars*-themed *Doom*. Or you can download a WAD that transforms the giant killer flesh-lumps into that jovial purple dinosaur Barney. There are Simpsons themes, *Army of Darkness* themes, and *Pulp Fiction* themes. There are even triple-X themes that switched out the normal walls for crude, pixelly hard core porn loops. Young guns could blast away bad guys with a rifle while wallpapers of porn stars undulated behind his kill. Experienced today, these porn *Dooms* feel like morbid folk art, depicting an ultimate death-fuck journey into the id.

Even creepier are the student-made mods that replaced *Doom*'s Martian outposts with accurate layouts of real schools and universities. Curious gamers can still point their browsers to the archives on doomworld.com, and download decade-old WADs that allow the player to decimate demons while wandering through the medieval colleges at Cambridge and Oxford. Or they could slaughter the denizens of certain obscure high schools: Unionville High School, outside of Toronto, remains available, as does Yarmouth High School of Yarmouth, Maine, whose programmer's commentary claims it is based on "original blueprints" of his school. The more technically minded may wish to "frag" demons while patrolling the virtual grounds of the Center for the Study of Optics and Lasers at the University of Central Florida, or the Engineering campus at Purdue University.

Doom's literally visceral quality, its splatterpunk gore, contributed greatly to the powerful effects of the game. Shoot an opponent, and a gush of red spray blossoms out from his chest. Corpses accumulate on floors in crimson heaps. If a fallen alien happens to land inside a door's frame, the portal closes with a disgusting *squish*. One particularly nasty monster looks like a giant lumbering lump of naked pink flesh, and requires numerous shotgun blasts to exterminate. With all these bleeding bodies, the *Doom* series is a particularly morbid enterprise.

In a blunt sense, *Doom* is about a brutal mastery over flesh; the gamer, whose muscles atrophied slowly as he sat near motionless at his PC for hours on end, became a disembodied gun, floating through tombs and destroying every warm body encountered. Film critic André Bazin once noted that death is but the victory of time, but *Doom* makes time malleable. So this highly addictive game was not just about killing time; it also felt like it killed death, at least momentarily. It was about stopping the flow of time, shutting out the rest of the world, in order to become enmeshed in the eternal, adrenaline-pumping Now of constant warfare. The death of enemies affirms one's own continued existence; even if defeated, the game can always start again.

In her 1965 essay "The Imagination of Disaster," Susan Sontag writes that atomic age sci-fi movies like *Godzilla* and *This Island Earth* provide "the immediate representation of the extraordinary: physical deformity and mutation, missile and rocket combat, toppling skyscrapers" and thereby invite viewers to "participate in the fantasy of living through one's death and more, the death of cities, the destruction of humanity itself." Thinking of *Doom*, it would be easy to argue that Sontag's observations are even truer for first-person video games. For here one may live through the fantasy of one's own death over and over again. Science fiction films attempt to absorb the viewer through a sense of awe—even if it is through the flawed sublime of giant monsters and otherworldly visitors. *Doom* does the same through first-person immersion, putting you in the action. The first time you find that seemingly unstoppable demon, you must experience death by its attack several times before you can determine how to survive. Each time you die, your character lets out a gurgled scream, and his point of view drops quickly to the ground.

Or maybe, Charles Bernstein suggests, "the death wish played out in these games is not a simulation at all." In "Play It Again Pac-Man," his prescient pre-*Doom* essay from 1991, Bernstein offers, "maybe it's time that's being killed or absorbed—real-life productive time that could be better 'spent' elsewhere." While killing time, the player feels active: moving through corridors, exploring buildings, destroying enemies. But much of these actions are in fact reactions, and in a larger sense, the player is being trained according to a larger narrative already deter-mined by the game's programming. It feels like free play, but the story cannot change; in fact, the game trains you to desire its rewards, to move up its levels, to find its treasures. Your char-acter's self-actualization is contingent on your abilities to obey the directives of the game, and in a larger sense, to complete the program's circuit, to satisfy its algorithms. It is a bondage that feels like freedom; you must get with the program to survive.

The game's designers couldn't have chosen a better name: "doom" is a bone-chilling Anglo-Saxon word that in its very pro-nunciation recalls the clanging of a death knell. It's a very old word, stretching back well before A.D. 1000; originally meaning an act of legal decree or pronouncement, it took on more omi-nous eschatological connotations of divine reckoning and inescapable fate as the centuries progressed. "Doomsday," for example, began as the earthy English term for the Day of Judg-ment; *Doom* arrived in an era that many saw as no less apoca-lyptic, as J. C. Herz notes in her 1997 pop-*Kulturschrift Joystick Nation.* "Even the word 'doom' is resonant," she writes, "Especially when you factor in all the scary technology lurking around the late twentieth century and the threat of rogue dictatorships blowing up Seattle with surplus Soviet nukes. In *Doom*, you get to resolve that sense of moral decay, political instability, and technophobia. You get to be global supercop, *Blade Runner*, and Oral Roberts, all rolled into one."

"You, and only you, are the hero," Herz writes. "No teamwork, no delegation, no profit sharing . . . We in America like this." And if *Doom* fans took on a role very much like the one-man vigilante badasses who busted their way through innumerable eighties action flicks, they were spurred on by an enemy that deserved certain death. Like the terrorists, Nazis, and KGB agents of other games and films, the alien enemies of *Doom* are incontrovertibly extermination-worthy, freeing the trigger-puller from any moral compunction. "You get to visit a place where there is no way to humanize the enemy because the enemy is, by definition, Evil," she offers. "Not just bad. Not misunderstood. Not the victim of childhood abuse, ethnic discrimination, faulty antidepressants, or low self-esteem . . . We all crave the perfect enemy. Political leaders employ squads of propagandists to create these monsters—the Evil Empire, Manuel Noriega, al-Qaddafi, Saddam Hussein—so that we can fly over and stomp on them. The makers of *Doom* understand how deeply satisfying this concept can be."

The perfect enemy is a component of the perfect war, or the Just War, the moral ideal that Herz alludes to in her litany of America's foreign bugaboos. The fact is that *Doom* and virtually all of its progeny fall into step with this framework, issuing forth an endless stream of zombies, robots, aliens, Nazis, robotic zombies, zombie aliens, and robot Nazis as oozing, creeping targets for righteous destruction. A few video games have played with reversing this notion, putting the player in the role of the bad guy. In Exidy's visually primitive 2-D arcade game from 1976 called *Death R*ace (inspired by the premise of Roger Corman's 1975 exploitation classic *Death Race 2000*), players earned points by running over little stick-figure people; even though the company claimed the victims were supposed to be "ghouls," the game cause, the first widespread public outcry against violence in video games. (Interestingly, Atari during this same period is said to have had an explicit policy that none of their games would include the destruction of recognizably human characters.) More recently, Bungie's highly narrative first-person shooter *Halo 2* (2005) takes a surprising turn midway, when suddenly the gamer is playing missions from the perspective of one of *Halo*'s main enemy race, the reptilian Covenant.

But *Doom* wasn't just about the lone hero, even if this is how many gamers experienced its play. In fact, one of its most notable features was the option for networking; up to four individuals could join forces, over a local area network or the higher-speed Internet connections available at colleges and institutions at the time, and blast the demonic forces using teamwork: the roots of the wildly popular practice of online gaming, via PC and console, available today. To win the game, players could think like police or soldiers, coordinating their efforts in ways that increased enemy death counts.

No wonder, then, that in 1997, a few Marines began to take *Doom* very seriously.

The Few, the Proud, the Networked

A decade after *Battlezone*, General Starry's vision of deploying video games proved remarkably prescient, if a little too ahead of its time; in the early 1980s, building thousands of stand-up arcade systems would have been exorbitantly expensive, even if they ran off of Atari's preexisting technology. Though theoretically cheaper than conventional trainers, *Army Battlezone* stand-ups would have still cost around $500,000 each.

With the fall of Soviet communism and the abrupt end of the Cold War, the Pentagon began to rethink the massive spending on essentially in-house technology development that it had pursued since the beginnings of World War II. New directives in the early 1990s stressed the need to run a more economically efficient military, a military that was run more along the lines of standard business practices, rather than the old reliance on Pentagon largess. Laws were passed that made it easier for private companies to sell supplies and goods to the military, encouraged competition for bidding, and reassigned lowest priority to programs unique to any one service branch. A more fiscally accountable military had all the more reason to interface with a global corporate culture.

But the PC revolution offered some new opportunities for drastic cost reduction. Heretofore, military computer simulations employed for training were expensive, relatively clunky affairs, whose programming focused primarily on reproducing pinpoint fidelity to realistic situations. An M1 tank trainer in the early eighties, for example, as produced by Chrysler or General Electric, would have run $6 to $7 million per unit. Running exclusively on high-priced, specialized graphics workstations, these ponderous tools were developed either in-house or by specialized military contracting firms. SIMNET came with a lower per-unit price tag—around $100,000 for each subsystem—but by the time that thousands of SIMNET trainers were in place, the whole program ran up to $850 million.

Another shortcoming with early military simulation was their lack of user-friendly engagement and "playability." In a nutshell: they were no fun, and this shortcoming was seen as inhibiting their training potential, particularly for a new generation who grew up with joysticks and controllers firmly in hand.

In the early nineties, the Marine Corps Modeling and Simulation Management Office had been given a new budgetary directive from the annual Marine Corps General Officers Symposium: find ways to use commercial, off-the-shelf software for internal training purposes. Never the most lavishly funded of America's Armed Forces, the Marines had a long tradition of making do with little, and the U.S. military in general had been attempting to move toward more streamlined fiscal models.

Marine Corps commandant Gen. Charles Krulak saw this fiscal necessity could be dovetailed with an increased emphasis on critical thinking that he saw as the future of the corps. Krulak wanted to "reach the stage where Marines come to work and spend part of each day talking about warfighting: learning to think, making decisions, and being exposed to tactical and operational issues," and he foresaw PC-based solutions for this goal. "The use of technological innovations," he wrote, "such as personal computer (PC)-based wargames, provide great potential for Marines to develop decision making skills."

The men at MCMSMO hit software stores and developed a study called the *Personal Computer Based Wargames Catalog*, which analyzed and reviewed over thirty military-themed strategy PC titles like *Operation Crusader, Patriot, Harpoon II,* and *Tigers on the Prowl* for usability as training systems. "The intent of this effort," they wrote in the *Catalog*, "was to examine the available wargames that are on the market and determine if any have the potential to teach a better appreciation for the art and science of war straight out of the box, with no modifications required." These *semper fi* tech-heads, however, found that nearly all these titles held scant value for their purposes. Though popular in military and gaming circles at the time, these PC battlers were little more than electronically enhanced versions of old tabletop war games. *Operation Crusader*, for example, employed kriegspeil-style hexagonal maps; *Harpoon II* updated the idea with late-twentieth-century radar displays that were nonetheless just as abstract. At best, these were games suited for learning command-level strategy or air defense, not the leatherneck-with-a-rifle warfare that is the Marines' forte. They were pastimes best suited for armchair generals and History Channel aficionados, not real-life Marines who needed practice working together, at ground level, on the battlefields of the future. "No wargame," the *Catalog* reports, "was capable of producing a robust simulated combat environment."

But one title in the *Wargames Catalog* proved fruitful. In 1997, Lieutenants Dan Snyder and Scott Barnett took advantage of *Doom II*'s modding capabilities to produce a new WAD with the needs of the Marines in mind. *Doom*'s world was stripped down and streamlined. The labyrinthine Martian dungeons were transformed into a sparse, dust-colored plain punctuated by small brick bunkers, foxholes, and barbed-wire barriers. Gone were the otherworldly aliens and demons, replaced by very human-looking opposing forces, clad in simple khaki military uniforms of a vaguely Communist/Nazi cut (according to technology historian Tim Lenoir, *Marine Doom*'s enemies were fashioned from scans of GI Joe action figures). The players' artillery choice was reduced to realistic weaponry (out with the electric plasma guns, in with the M-16 A1 assault rifle, the M-249 squad automatic weapon, and M-67 fragmentations grenades); life-refreshing power-ups disappeared. With lower life levels and no chance to raise them, the player died quickly, after only a couple of hits. Thus was born *Marine Doom* (also known as *Marine*

Corps Doom or simply *MCDoom*). It was *Army Battlezone* for the PC generation, a boots-on-the-ground combat simulator.

With *Marine Doom*, two pairs of Marines could engage in net-worked play in order to practice teamwork operations as a standard four-man fire team. *Marine Doom* didn't train for marksmanship; it trained for cooperation. The teams could set up fields of fire, conduct flanking maneuvers, and enact "leapfrog tactics" in which some team members pin down an enemy with gunfire while others advance ahead. "While weapons behavior is not extremely accurate," *Marine Doom*'s Web site read, "sound tactical employment of these models should give the desired effect." Old-style simulators had cost hundreds of thousands of dollars to do similar things: *Marine Doom* cost a mere $49.95 for the original game, which was then altered with Snyder and Barnett's marine1.wad freeware file. The *Marine Doom* WAD was soon trading furiously through numerous *Doom*-dedicated BBSes and online forums, and quickly became in turn cannibalized for the fantastical WADs of other modders.

In early 1997, official word about *Marine Doom* went out in the January 27th ALMAR, a newswire sent by the commandant to all Marines worldwide, along with news that jarheads would soon be permitted to play the game on government computers, as long as they adhered to copyright restrictions. "As programs are developed, I challenge you to seek opportunities to include an element of stress," General Krulak recommended. "Decisions made in war must frequently be made under physical and emotional stress. Our mental exercises in peacetime should replicate some of the same conditions. Leaders can generate stress by placing time limits on decisions, by conducting games immediately following a strenuous PT session or forced march, or requiring decisions during a period of sleep deprivation."

For a brief moment, the *Marine Doom* teams were tech-world rock stars. *Marine Doom* racked up scads of attention, both within the military, where it was seen as an intriguing innovation, and in the mainstream press, who saw in it the seeds of some cyberpunked future. *Wired Magazine* gave the mod its April 1997 cover, with a headline that read "Doom Goes to War: the Marines are looking for a few good games," over an image of the scowling face of *Doom*'s Space Marine, clad in twentieth-century brown camo helmet. But despite the hype and rock-bottom cost, *Marine Doom* was never an official part of training, and was never implemented on a widespread basis; its developers eventually left active duty to pursue commercial software jobs. Snyder, for example, worked as a consultant on GT Interactive's 1998 game *Nam*, a Vietnam War–themed shooter that boasted realistic weaponry.

More importantly, *Marine Doom* signaled a new interest in the use of commercial games for official military training. A couple of years later, Spectrum Holobyte (best known for importing *Tetris* to the U.S.) modified the PC game *Falcon 4.0*, a networked flight simulator, for use in training real F-15 pilots.

The U.S. Naval Academy shanghaied Electronic Art's *Jane's Fleet Command* for training purposes; the game was developed by Sonalysts, who in turn have a long history of military commissions, and needed no modification for the Navy's purposes. In later years, Novalogic modified *Delta Force 2* to train for the Army's Land Warrior system, the Navy taught a modified version of *Microsoft Flight Simulator*, and Ubisoft worked with the Army to redesign *Tom Clancy's Rainbow Six: Rogue Spear* for urban combat training.

Mäk Technologies, a defense contracted software film founded by former SIMNET designers, specialized in desktop-based simulation trainers, producing two games for the Marines that were also released commercially: *Spearhead*, a multiplayer tank sim, and *Marine Expeditionary Unit 2000,* a strategy title. *MEU 2000* "isn't about influencing young people's view of the military, but it can be helpful to people who want to learn more about the military," the game's lead designer, Patrick Brennan, told *Gaming News Network* in 1998. "We have discussed the recruiting and public relations potential of a game like *MEU 2000* with the Marines."

In 2000, the Joint Chiefs of Staff commissioned Rival Interactive to create a game called *Joint Force Employment*, a turn-based strategy game to simulate how officers might react to a terrorist crisis. Its title references the modern military concept of "jointness," or cooperation across all military branches. A year later, Rival released the game to the public in two parts,

Real War and *Real War: Rogue States.* In the game, players battle a fictitious group called the Independence Liberation Army, a terrorist outfit who has obtained weapons of mass destruction. Its distributor, Simon & Schuster, attempted to drum up sales after the advent of September 11th; free give-aways with the game included a copy of Sun Tzu's *The Art of War* and cell phone ringtones that bleeped "America the Beautiful." "It's a very pro-American game that shows how powerful the U.S. military is," a Simon & Schuster Interactive spokesman told the *Hollywood Reporter.* "And it's cathartic to blow up terrorists."

Trashed by gaming reviewers as clunky and outdated, the *Real War* series bombed. But by the time the War on Terror rolled around, both the military and the commercial sector were working on much bigger projects together.

An early game of war from ancient Egypt. Illustration by James Fotopoulos, adapted from a satirical papyrus, from 1100 B.C., now held at the British Museum.

Korean Minister of War Yun-Woong-Niel plays a game of Go in this image from a 1904 stereogram by Underwood & Underwood. (Courtesy of Library of Congress Prints and Photographs Division)

At I/ITSEC 2004 in Orlando: *America's Army* adapted for use as a convoy trainer.

I/ITSEC attendees try the latest urban combat simulator from Dynamic Animation Systems, designed with a Middle Eastern theme.

Dynamic Animation Systems decorated its "I/ITSEC booth" with this illustration: a melding of game-style graphics and War on Terror bravado.

Virtual Iraq, seen in a Flatworld prototype at the Institute for Creative Technologies, USC.

Recreating realistic natural radiance in Paul Debevec's workshop at ICT.

Another Flatworld prototype, this one viewable in 3-D when seen through polarized lenses.

Two screenshots from *Operation Secret Storm* (1991), created for the NES by Color Dreams. It was one of the earliest video games to depict a contemporary war. (Courtesy of Vance Kozik, StarDot Technologies)

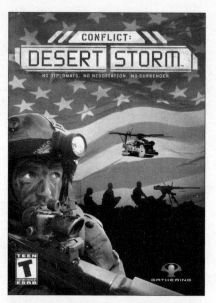

History as battleground: box cover art for *Conflict: Desert Storm* (2002) and *Vietcong: Purple Haze* (2004). (Courtesy of Take-Two Interactive Software)

Cheapo Chinese handheld *Laden vs. USA* (2001), released weeks after September 11th. (Photo by James Fotopoulos)

An Arab perspective: poster for *UnderSiege* (2005). (Courtesy of Radwan Kasmiya, Afkarmedia)

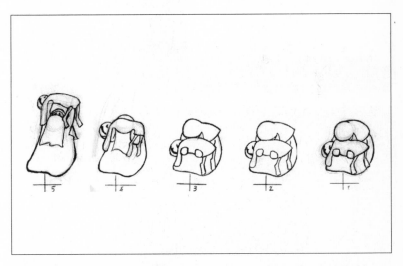

Animation sketch for a mourning villager in *September 12th, a toy world* (2003). (Courtesy of Gonzalo Frasca, Newsgaming.com)

The website for Jason Huddy's game *Blood of Bin Laden* (2003). (Courtesy of Jason Huddy)

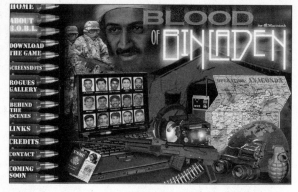

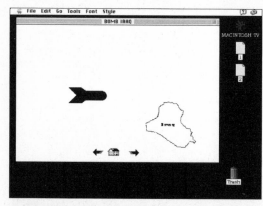

Two artworks by Cory Arcangel from 2006: *Bomb Iraq* and *MiG-29 fighter and clouds*, installed at Pace-Wildenstein Gallery, New York City. (Courtesy of Pace-Wildenstein Gallery)

PART FOUR
THE DREAM WAR

LINKING ENTERTAINMENT
AND DEFENSE

And for pleasure, there was the simulator, the most perfect video game that he had ever played. Teachers and students trained him, step by step, in its use. At first, not knowing the awesome power of the game, he had played only at the tactical level, controlling a single fighter in continuous maneuvers to find and destroy an enemy. . . . It was exhilarating at last to have such control over the battle, to be able to see every point of it.

—Orson Scott Card, *Ender's Game*, 1985

Virtual reality opens new spaces for exploration, colo-
nization, and exploitation, returning to a mythic time
when there were worlds without limits and resources
beyond imagining.

—Henry Jenkins, "Nintendo and New World Travel Writing," 1995

In late March 2003, *Fox News* anchor Brit Hume interviewed
Secretary of State Colin Powell, less than a week into the U.S.
invasion of Iraq. The national mood was queasy. The tense
lead-up to the invasion had threaded through the color-coded
emergencies, duct tape mania, global protests, and terrorist-
produced video messages that comprised the year and a half
of events since the destruction of the World Trade Center.
Already fine-tuned into both a barometer and instrument of
the national anxiety, television dove into the Iraq war with
immersive twenty-four-hour coverage; the pyrotechnic bombastics of shock-and-awe quickly switched to the thickly pix-
eled mobile cameras of embedded reporters, providing
unprecedented real-time visions of battle that were both chill-
ingly immediate and strangely unreal, like Webcams peeping
into an outer circle of Hell. Now, accounts of troop deaths and
American POWs began to punctuate press reports, the stock
market descended, and even conservative news outlets began
speculating whether America's strategy might have been
deficient.

Hume asked Powell to take the pulse of the moment. "Well

Brit," he replied, "people have to understand that this isn't a video game. It's a war. A real war."

In its very offhandedness, Powell's comment pointed to how commonplace the comparison of modern warfare to video games had become. Whether consciously or not, he echoed his former commander, General Norman Schwarzkopf, who had made a similar statement more than a decade earlier, during the first Gulf War. In a press conference in Riyadh, Saudi Arabia, on February 28, 1991, Schwarzkopf reminded the press corps that "the kind of thing that's going on out on that battlefield right now is not a Nintendo game. It is a tough battlefield where people are risking their lives at all times, and great heroes out there, and we ought to all be very, very proud of them."

From its beginnings, the Gulf War had been dubbed "the first Nintendo War" by the media, and Schwarzkopf wished to disabuse them of such notions. Nevertheless, the metaphor proved incredibly sticky—so much so that, years later, many seemed to think that Schwarzkopf himself had coined the phrase. It was a perfect expression for a war that appeared on television screens as night raids resembling the 2-D light blips of *Arkanoid* or *Tetris*, and fought through an increased array of electronic interfaces. It was a war that touted the so-called "surgical strike," enabled by superior American technological know-how.

"For a generation of soldiers, sailors and fliers raised in the era of the computer chip," the *Boston Globe* wrote in January 1991, "this has been their kind of war: the Nintendo War. Indeed, many of the screens that military operators use to launch weapons and spy on air traffic look eerily like something plucked from a video arcade." The *Globe* writer invokes the image of the video arcade, not the more domesticated home computer. Even as late as the early nineties, the popular vision of the arcade remained that of a seedy, violent, and immature realm of games like *Street Fighter II* and *Mortal Kombat.* In the public imagination —and in run-down areas of recession-era cities nationwide—the arcade remained an overly testosteroned, juvie-populated zone of cheap cologne, gang fashions, and sketchy dudes selling butterfly knives to middle-school roughnecks. Eerie indeed.

From Schwarzkopf's to Powell's war in Iraq, Americans became acquainted with a far greater array of digital technologies—not just the rise of the Internet and the spread of increasingly powerful home computers, but also several generations of video game console systems, each more powerful than its predecessor. Game graphics fleshed out from boxy diagrams to rounded bodies; 2-D scrolling adventures gave way to first-person wanderings through unpredictable landscapes. Even the presentation of television news became more an Internetish, gamelike info-panel. What were all those creeping news items, stock tickers, and information geegaws that began to crowd the screens of CNN and Fox News but a kind of heads-up display for the state of the world, keeping tabs on the global equivalents of energy, ammo, lives and the score? "Any time death is imminent, life is exciting," Andy Rooney kvetched to his fellow predigital geriatrics on the March 30, 2003, edition of

60 Minutes (and unwittingly evoked the thrill of games like *Doom* and *Halo*) "and we're watching this war as though it was a video game. On television, it's hard to know where to look to find out what you want to know. There are pictures on top of pictures, moving print on top of those. There's more than the eye can see, or the brain comprehend."

But though generals and pundits may wish draw lines in the sand between warfare and video games, a closer look at developments in the world of military technology for training and recruitment in the last five years reveals a very different relationship. As the digitization of war evolved along with the new media boom, its interfaces and visual logic became increasingly homologous to what civilians might find on their PC or Xbox. Simulation has become big business, and the worlds of entertainment and defense have entered a new era of synergy. Early one-off efforts like *Army Battlezone* and *Marine Doom* blossomed into full-blown collaborations among game companies, Hollywood, and military contractors.

Press Start to Continue

In one corner of a football-field-sized convention floor crammed with corporate display booths, representatives from VirTra Systems stand at the entranceway to their company's exhibition tent. Different videotaped military and security training scenarios play inside, unfolding within a virtual environment formed by a series of synchronous, interactive projections covering five walls of the hexagonal structure. The stories' images, for the most part, aren't computer-generated. They contain real actors, recorded on low-budget sets or outdoor locations, the no-name types one might see in a corporate training video, complete with costumes and ersatz facial hair. A rep walks to the center of the near-circle of giant video images, clutching a realistic-looking laser pistol, as one of several pre-programmed narratives begins: An Al Qaeda terrorist has taken an American engineer hostage, and the rep needs to shoot the bearded villain down as soon as a pair of doors fly open on one of the video screens. The rep's laser pistol fires loudly, but misses its mark, hitting instead a pack of explosives strapped to the terrorist's chest. The walls glow with a fiery, CGI blast—the mechanized floor, in fact, vibrates like an enormous video game controller—and the scenario ends. The whole event has taken less than two and a half seconds. The other rep turns to the name-tagged conventioneers clustered around the tent's opening. "See, this is what our military and law enforcement have to deal with on a daily basis," he declares.

"Now, you can also use this to enhance the experience," the VirTra rep continues, fastening a thick, black device around his waist. The "threat-fire belt," he explains, issues a stunning electric shock to the trainee if he or she is "hit" by the imaginary bullet of a virtual assailant, who might appear anywhere on the semicircular screen. "If you get hit in the back, trust me, you'll remember it. This one will bring you to your knees. The whole idea is to fight through the pain, and keep on going, just the way that you've been trained." Enveloped inside massive video screens and booming surround sound, the trainee is placed within the story in a viscerally literal way. If implemented, perhaps VirTra's pain trainer will precipitate a new medical condition: pre traumatic stress disorder, arriving before the war fighter even hits the battlefield.

Later, another participant—this time, a college-age National Guardsman in uniform—dons the threat-fire belt and enters a different scenario. He plays the role of a police officer who has stopped a drunk driver. Onscreen, an actor playing the driver exits her car, staggering and jabbering slurred nonsense, then begins fumbling through her handbag, muttering about looking for her license. "Ma'am, put your hands up. Put your hands where I can see 'em!" the soldier orders the video image sternly, "Ma'am, I *will* use lethal force!" The woman stumbles to the left of her car, gesticulating and protesting her innocence, and the soldier in turn keeps his weapon aimed at her image. Suddenly, a loud, cracking BANG issues from the soldier's right: an armed man had appeared without warning outside of the soldier's line of vision, and shot him. The soldier grabs the threat-fire belt around his waist as it zaps his body with an extremely real shock. "I think it's a little bit better to feel a little bit of pain when you get shot so you can learn from it and not want to get shot again," he says afterward, with a casual smile. "It's a little easy to be Rambo when it doesn't hurt."

VirTra was one of hundreds of private contractors and military agencies showing off the latest in media-based training systems at the December 2004 edition of I/ITSEC, the cumbersomely named Interservice/Industry Training, Simulation, and Education Conference held annually in Orlando, Florida. I/ITSEC exists to bring together the different branches of the U.S. military, related government agencies, private contractors, and academia to showcase new and future developments in simulation-based training—military lingo for the technology-enhanced, serious-minded make-believe that provides the cornerstone of modern preparation for battle. I/ITSEC began three decades ago, when simulation training meant mechanical airplane cockpit mock-ups with blinking electronic lights, or live play-acted war games of the red-versus-blue variety. Way back in the 1980s, it introduced the first versions of SIMNET to the military-industrial community.

Such antique practices have now merged with cutting-edge developments from the worlds of science and entertainment. Today, attendees are more likely to engage with something along the lines of VirTra's immersive virtual theater: the souped-up, grown-up cousins of video games, tailor-made to teach the new media generation how to fight America's war on terror.

War on the Floor

At first glance, the convention floor seems like a dot-com era throwback. Elaborately decorated walk-through displays pack a hall the size of a football field, each stuffed with monitors, flyers, and logo-printed giveaway trinkets. Some bear familiar names—Saab, Boeing, Hewlett-Packard, Silicon Graphics. Sound tracks to corporate videos bleed into one another, punctuated by newscaster-cool voice-overs, corny synths, and adrenaline-pumping guitar riffs. Many representatives wear matching team outfits: One group mingles in white lab coats; another in Red Sox jerseys, commemorating the team's recent World Series win. A smiling female booth staffer offers ice cream in exchange for dropping a business card in a fishbowl, as a polo-shirted man silently creeps by on a Segway scooter.

But it's 2004, not 2000, so the business at hand is fighting war and defending the homeland. Suits are as plentiful as desert camo; some displays are swathed in army-green netting. Near the floor's entrance, a giant plasma screen shows a pilot's-eye view of a bombing run over a computer-generated desert landscape, where digital explosions blossom to the tune of Led Zeppelin's "Whole Lotta Love." In one booth, a female model marches in place, wearing a blue leotard covered with motion-tracking white dots. Above her, a real-time computer-generated image of a male soldier follows the movements of her body.

A company called Dynamic Animation Systems shows off its urban-combat-themed marksmanship trainer prototype in six shooting-gallery style stalls equipped with video projectors. In each stall, men in suits or uniforms pick up laser rifles and blast away at CGIed Arab insurgents, who jump out from behind cars and rubble in a digital mock-up of an Iraqi city, complete with fading posters of Saddam Hussein on the sides of buildings. To the casual observer, the trainer's graphics would seem indistinguishable from those of the latest Iraq-themed game for Playstation or Xbox—and how cool would it be if home console systems came with full-size artillery? A woman in jeans and a pink shirt grabs a gun and starts picking off hooded villains with ruthless precision. "Oh man, she is cold!" laughs a soldier standing behind her.

A few paces away, a grinning man who could be Dick Cheney's stunt double—late-fiftyish, balding, dark-blue suit and tie—perches atop a mock armored vehicle, inside another dome of video projections, machine-gunning down computer-generated terrorists as a barren, sand-colored landscape rolls around him. Smoke pours from his mounted gun, and real metal shells fall onto the carpeted floor. "They use real blanks instead of an air pump," explains a booth staffer, "so that he can get the full range of motion, and feel a realistic recoil." In a nearby display made to look like half of a two-story home, crafted from raw plywood, two teenagers sway silently in virtual-reality helmets, waving rifles. On the screens positioned above their heads, the crowd can see the fantasy environment the teens are patrolling inside their minds. Visitors pour out of an enclosed metal chamber, following a taste of patrolling the desert in a virtual Humvee; they smile and laugh, as if they've just gotten off a roller coaster.

To a blue-state civilian outsider, the scene might at first seem surreal—or, perhaps, all too real: the ultimate convergence of digital entertainment and the war on terror, a vision worthy of Paul Verhoeven or David Cronenberg, a dystopic sci-fi cliché come to life. And if the I/ITSEC conventioneers appeared unusually buoyant at a time when the ultimate outcome of war in Iraq remained uncertain, it may be because business was booming. An estimated 16 percent of the current U.S. defense spending goes toward training, and the dollar amount has escalated sharply since 9/11. In 2000, about $3 billion was spent annually on the MS&T (modeling, simulation, and training) industry; now, the figure is closer to $6 billion, thanks to increased demand from both domestic security and conflicts abroad. By all accounts, the U.S. armed forces today devote far more time, money, and research on soldier training than any other military in the world, and as a result, support a nexus of academic, corporate, and military interests collaboratively devoted to pushing new media technologies forward.

Military-industrial complex? The concept seems so quaintly Cold War, so hopelessly last century. Journalists and academics have bandied about a number of new catchphrases to describe the burgeoning world of simulation technologies. The most successful would be one coined by cyberpunk author Bruce Sterling in the early nineties: the "military-entertainment complex." *Megatrends* futurist John Naisbitt proposed "Military-Nintendo Complex" in his 1999 book *High Tech, High Touch*—despite the fact that Nintendo is probably the only game company that does not seem to have ever been involved in military affairs; others have used "militainment" or "the military-industrial society." Certain leftist circles prefer political scientist James Der Derian's term: the "Military-Industrial-Media-Entertainment Network," or MIME-NET, expounded in his 2001 postmodernist road trip through this brave new military world, *Virtuous War*. Therein, the author finds that his digestion of Continental philosophers like Paul Virilio, Guy Debord, and Jean Baudrillard seems to have especially prepared him to face the future shocks dealt by his visits to I/ITSEC and elsewhere. "I drew from some thinkers who well understood the seductive powers of simulations," Der Derian writes, "who consider hyperbole to be a *pragmatic* response to the hyperreal."

Indeed, I/ITSEC would be a perfect opportunity for any Europhile thinker who wished to mourn the collapse of the real and the simulated, and it offers numerous opportunities such a figure to opine on *la folie américaine* to boot. One company called Strategic Operations Tactical Training gave out DVDs to press while promoting their facilities: an eleven-acre outdoor film studio in San Diego, where they promise, as the company's Web site touts, "the 'magic of Hollywood' to simulate a real world training environment for tomorrow's threat" and "the application of modern day movie making techniques combined with Simunition® to create a sense of realism for your training needs." Their DVD shows clips of bloody playacted battles performed in the California scrub: men and women dressed as Middle Eastern villagers run as U.S. troops and tribal gunmen clash amid the sounds of gunfire and explosions. In an episode focusing on "Combat Trauma Training," a mixture of hired actors and actual Marines can be seen in the footage; a number of freshly wounded troops lie on the ground, awaiting medical evacuation, their faces and leg stumps covered in fake blood and ash as they pretend to writhe in pain. Some of these wounded, the company's rep says, were real-life veterans who had lost legs in combat. Strategic Operations' press kit, emblazoned with HYPER-REALISTIC TRAINING in red military-stencil lettering, includes a testimonial from an unnamed Marine Corps battalion commander: "The wounds created by the make-up artists were so realistic," he states, "that one amputee role player, that was simulating having his leg blown off, was stuck with an IV by a corpsman who believed it to be a real injury caused by a training explosive gone awry."

Orlando Magic

The technologies that shape our culture have always been pushed forward by war: not just computers and video games, but cell-phones, transistors, microwave ovens, and even canned food all emerged from wartime research. In the long term, then, Orlando may be shaping our collective futures more than Hollywood or Silicon Valley. But what kind of future is it calling forth?

Drive through the city's superwide, highwaylike streets, crammed with gaudy, oversized buildings mostly thrown up in the last decades: an limitless sprawl of gigantic chain stores and minimalls, everywhere lined by imported palm trees, all so sparkling new that they make California seem superannuated in comparison. Turn on the car radio, and the stations alternate between born-again Christian programming and dirty-South hip-hop, conservative talk radio and Latin pop. Then go back inside the gargantuan Orange County Convention Center, revisit I/ITSEC, and watch teenagers tear through imaginary bullets, firing machine guns at life-size and computer-generated Iraqis.

The conference's Orlando location bears significance. Defense and entertainment are among the most robust industries in Florida, which has seen significant economic growth in recent years, much of it centered around the state's "high-tech corridor" in central Florida, which includes the Army's office for Simulation, Training, and Instrumentation Command (known as PEO STRI, formerly STRICOM), the University of Central Florida's Institute for Simulation and Training, and Lockheed Martin Missiles and Fire Control, which employs more than 7,000 Floridians. Over a hundred firms are tenants at the Central Florida Research Park, the majority of them top military contractors like Anteon, Boeing, CAE Systems Flight & Simulation Training, Cubic Defense Systems, Excalibur Defense Systems, General Dynamics, L-3 Communications, Saab Training, Raytheon, Titan, Sonalysts, and United Defense, as well as individual training and simulation offices representing the Army, Navy, Air Force, and Marines. Not far afield are Walt Disney

World, EPCOT, Sea World, and Universal Studios. It's no wonder that I/ITSEC attracted more than 1,800 representatives from over forty nations, eager to check up on what the world's most technology-heavy military was up to.

"The question is how to integrate [defense] with the world of entertainment," former Disney animator Bob Allen told the *Boston Globe* in 2003. Allen's production company, Integrity Arts & Technology, created a simulation trainer called *Battle Stations* for the Navy; the concept reportedly emerged out of a meeting at Starbucks between a Navy reservist, Allen, and a Universal Studios exec. "There is an intuitive sense," Allen says, "that this will be the next big thing."

"Modeling, simulation, and training" is cited as one of the six target industries whose growth is supported and fostered by the Florida High Tech Corridor Council, a consortium of academic and governmental interests established in 1996. For example, one of the council's initiatives, the Modeling, Simulation, and Training techCAMP, brings in local middle and high school educators to inform them of the many Florida job opportunities available in the field, from defense to theme parks. Their visit includes tours of Universal Studios' *Shrek, Jimmy Neutron,* and *Spiderman* themed rides as well as a comprehensive overview of the military simulation sector. "I didn't realize how much engineering and technology was involved in the theme park industry," the council's April 2005 press release quotes a visiting high school teacher as purportedly saying. "And I didn't realize that Orlando was the center of simulation and in need of employees."

University of Central Florida professor Christopher Stapleton was on hand at I/ITSEC, representing his school's Media Convergence Laboratory. Located within UCF's Intitute for Simulation and Training, the Media Convergence Laboratory researches "new ways of making memories that will last a lifetime," according to its Web site; it's "about making creative leaps in experiential media innovation." In other words, it's a research lab for interactive virtual reality systems, the kind of immersive digital environments that not only draw elements from the technology of both video games and military simulation, but could be seen as the future of both forms.

Stapleton is a soft-voiced, wide-eyed man with a freckled face—not the type you might expect to run into at a hard-edged military conference. Before his position as director of the lab, his résumé included stints producing entertainment, marketing, and educational technology for clients like Universal Studios, Nickelodeon, Disney, and Sanrio, the Japanese company known worldwide as the purveyors of Hello Kitty. On the lab's Web site, scroll a cursor over his head shot, and it changes to a black-and-white photo of himself as a smiling boy. "Central Florida," he explains "is the world capital of experiential entertainment." Here, he continues, "you're going to find the best, most intensive entertainment that you experience in 3D. Real-life, real-time interactivity. The headquarters for the simulation

The Dream War   191

research for Navy, Army, Marine Corps, and Air Force are here."
From Stapleton's standpoint, events like I/ITSEC are only the
merest beginnings of the potential technological synergy that
could be unleashed among these fields.

During and after World War II, the Pentagon funded research
labs at MIT and Stanford; a new historical moment is visible in
the underwriting of the Media Convergence Lab, whose partners
range from PEO STRI, the Office of Naval Research, and the
Naval Postgraduate School's MOVES Institute, to Universal Studios, Canon, and Nickelodeon. This melding of corporate, academic, and defense interests could be seen as one "convergence"
of the lab's name; the other is the many forms of media and technology that come together to create the various forms of imaginary theater under construction. As a result, Stapleton has his
digital fingers in any number of virtual pies. "We're doing experiential media with mixed reality for experiential movie trailers,"
Stapleton says. "We're working with marketing for car dealers.
We're applying it to marketing and tourism. We just had a field
test at the Orlando Science Center, where we had a dinosaur
exhibit come to life with mixed reality and computer graphics
and physical exhibits, with interactive games within the physical
space with virtual content. So we're playing to the info-educa-
tional market, which is larger than the home game market."

Though diverse in scope, the Media Convergence Lab has an
I/ITSEC presence because it's also deeply involved in military
applications for simulation technology. One of its major projects,

MR MOUT, explores ways to use "mixed reality" to train for MOUT, or Military Operations in Urban Terrain—the kind of fighting that American troops see in Baghdad, Falluja, or Kabul, a corollary to the age of asymmetrical warfare. "The future of war is going to be in urban terrain," Stapleton says. "With the superior military force of the US, I don't think any opposing force is going to go out in the field and start fighting us. They'd be dead. The only advantage they do have is in urban terrain, where it's very difficult to do the analysis process, because the American military approach to fighting is you want to minimize casualties, and maximize efficiency."

MR MOUT involves a combination of virtual realities and physical architecture. With tiny specialized VR headset in place, a trainer wanders through a theatrical set of imitation build- ings whose doors and windows are blue screens. The helmet chromakeys three-dimensional images onto those blue spaces, creating the illusion of an environment beyond the set. To the outside observer, the soldier moving through MR MOUT looks like an actor in an *American Playhouse* rendition of *Lawn- mower Man.* "With real and virtual reality intertwined, it becomes the closest thing we have to the concept of the holodeck," the Lab's MR MOUT Web site states, citing the virtual reality chamber seen in the series *Star Trek: The Next Genera- tion.* "It is like a theme park on steroids."

Unlike the mythic MIT hackers of the 1960s, Stapleton does not see the U.S. military as merely a ponderous source of funding, some kind of unwitting cash cow for subversive nerds with a yen for creative exploration at their employer's expense. Rather, he sees the military themselves as active partners and technological visionaries in their own right, at least in the field of simulation. According to Stapleton, working with the military means being involved with the forefront of simulation technology, having access to projects far more advanced and forward-looking than anything happening in the pure entertainment sector. "I'm from the entertainment industry," Stapleton explains. "I spent twenty years doing Broadway, theme parks and so forth." And from his experience, Stapleton dismisses the popular notion that America's cutting-edge entertainment industry—whether Hollywood or the gaming world—represents the apex of experiential technologies. "I think the entertainment industry is the most reluctant adopter of innovation, and they are still conceptually in the dark ages."

Stapleton says he sometimes needs to explain this to military types, who go ga-ga over the exciting graphics produced by Microsoft, Sony, or any number of game developers. Commercial games, he says, are "really good at the visualization. So of course the military people come up to me and say, 'Oh the game industry, it looks so cool! Why does it look so cool?' And I ask them, how many artists do you hire? Because engineers and scientists have been developing military simulation, and the entertainment industry has been getting artists. On the same token, artists are hacking away, making it look beautiful, and it looks great and so forth, but what's under the hood is really what's going to matter in the future." Modern-day labs like Stapleton's seek to bring digital artists and war fighters together; it's the kind of high-paying synergy that art schools might not tell you about. While military technology may make simulations realistic, Stapleton says, it's the artists of the entertainment world who can make them compelling.

Even if Stapleton thinks military technology could learn from entertainment's visual whiz-bang, he argues that it's the entertainment side of things that's holding the technology back from its ultimate possibilities. Hollywood is only interested in the most superficial aspects of image generation, and the game industry, he says, "is not looking at is the real science and art beyond the obvious reactive, thumb-twitching kind of experience that has some kind of titillation to it. And so that's why I transferred from the entertainment industry into working with military research, because military are the people who are asking the tough questions, and the deep questions that will matter twenty, thirty years from now."

"The military," Stapleton stresses, "are actually the visionaries of experiential media."

All but War Is Simulation

Even if Stapleton's team is busy perfecting technologies of interest to both the Navy and Nickelodeon, it doesn't mean that the interactive trainers on view at I/ITSEC are mere super-sized playthings. At least that's the view of Michael Macedonia, the affable and boyish fortysomething technology officer of PEO STRI, the Army's Orlando-based office for Simulation, Training, and Instrumentation Command, who wants to stress that the large-scale shoot-'em-ups on display at I/ITSEC are definitely not just kids' toys. PEO STRI's promotional materials, distributed at the conference, display the office's name in futuristic, silver lettering, reminiscent of the title design for the *Terminator* films. The office's emblem is a round shield: green cartoon soldier's torso joined to a lightning bolt are set against a red, white, and blue target; underneath, a stylized laurel wreath bears the motto ALL BUT WAR IS SIMULATION.

Macedonia is obsessed with training through simulation; he is a man whose career is clearly his passion. "We used to say in the army, the only two things we do before war is we train and maintain," he says. "When we go to war, we train and we fight. Essentially it never stops, it's like an endless cycle." PEO STRI's motto, he explains, "sort of sums up the philosophy . . . Everything is preparation for war. Everything we do is practice for war—it's getting ready for combat. And until that point, it's all simulation; it's still an abstraction. Until you're in combat, it's all in your head. It's virtual. And the only real war is really what you experience in combat." The trick, then, is for training to approximate war as closely as possible: the ultimate goal must be perfect simulation, and therefore getting inside those soldiers' "heads" is key.

With a round, impish face and an ever-ready grin, Macedonia
is a busy man not only at I/ITSEC; he often represents the Army
at any number of conferences devoted to what academics and
others are beginning to call "serious games"–the use of video
games for education and training. Raised in a military family
(his father, Ray Macedonia, was instrumental in reviving the
use of war gaming at the Army War College in the 1960s), Macedonia holds a Ph.D. in computer science. He is a Gulf War veteran and essentially a veteran of the War on Terror: he was
inside the Pentagon on September 11, 2001, when terrorists
killed 125 people by crashing American Airlines Flight 77 into
the building. In conversation, he may quote Herbert Marcuse or
Plato, or explain the moral significance of Pixar's animated film
The Incredibles. He seems to gravitate toward movies that cele-
brate the national character. "I used to be the president of the
film society at West Point," he says. "We had James Cagney come
up, for *Yankee Doodle Dandy*. We had George C. Scott come up,
for his role in *Patton*. We had a John Ford series. I learned so
much about John Ford movies, and I learned that they're really
about the Irish immigrant experience in America."

While espousing a cultivated love of art and entertainment, of
culture both high and pop, Macedonia argues that military simulations and video games are essentially different. "First of all,"
he sound bites, "the object is not to entertain you, but to train
you." He continues, "The reality is, if you really look at some of
these things, they would actually be quite boring to your average

game-player," noting that many simulations are created to train for unglamorous, mundane skills, like machine maintenance. "I've been in a lot of flight simulators, and the thing is you realize, they're just like the plane. And if you don't know how to fly, you're going to crash it. So it's not an amusement ride."

Macedonia brings up the case of *Full Spectrum Warrior*, a much-publicized video game developed by the Army with the help of a commercial gaming company. A popular, consumer-friendly version was released for Xbox in the summer of 2004, to critical acclaim and healthy sales. A related but different form is currently used as a console-based tactical trainer within the Army. "If you play the Army version—which is the only one that the Army endorses, by the way—it's actually very realistic, but it's really hard. People complain that they get killed in five minutes, and can't figure it out. Well that's because we're trying to get as realistic as possible. It's about training, and so it's about making it hard."

Such high-tech training, Macedonia contends, is part of the modern military's post-Vietnam paradigm. Before 1970, the U.S. Army "trained through blood," he says. "Technology for training was considered expensive. People were cheap. Essentially, we could draft them and send them over, and train them for six weeks, and send them into combat, and if they survived their first combat patrols, they were going to live for the rest of the year. That attitude changed dramatically with Vietnam. They got back and essentially said, no we're smarter than this, we're not going to do this again. We're going to invest in the technology for training. And we're going to go with volunteers and not draft people against their will." A new emphasis on training, then, coincided with Westmoreland's vision of the electronic battle-field. Both ideas would ensure a military that would, in theory, yield fewer U.S. casualties, encourage a more dedicated force, and by extension, garner public support more easily.

But even if military simulation and commercial gaming are different species, Macedonia sees one important area of conflu-ence. "Essentially entertainment and games, that is, entertain-ment and training have an intersection: it's about making memories. It's fascinating now what we're learning about the human brain." He cites the work of UC San Diego neurologist V. S. Ramachandran, the author of a book called *Phantoms of the Brain*, a rumination on how the mind functions through exam-ining brain disorders. "One thing he says is that we are our memories," Macedonia says, grinning with the wide-eyed enthu-siasm of an academic enamored by a beautiful idea. "And we don't think about that too often every day, but you see that evi-dence in Alzheimer's patients, in stroke patients. So a lot of what we're trying to do in training is creating memories. Memo-ries that last forever."

There, Macedonia believes, lies the true overlap with enter-tainment, and art. "The ultimate artist," he continues, "is some-body who leaves you with a memory long after—'Rosebud' all that sort of stuff. V. S. Ramachandran says that we have this virtual reality program in our head. I thought that was interesting. In the training world, we try to create a virtual reality around the virtual reality program in our head. And I think in a sense is games try to do the same thing, not realizing it. It's not intentional. That is, we're trying to mess with that program a little bit, so you remember long afterward *that* experience. So that when you're confronted with it in combat, or some other particular situation, you recall that." He talks about the birth of literature as the beginnings of a new kind of memory. "You can almost say that the Greeks were the developers of simulation," says Macedonia. "The oral tradition of Homer and the story with the war of the Trojans," he says, could be seen as "an experience that was really passing down knowledge, and understanding of not only history, but war fighting."

Creating memories: an unintentionally disturbing phrase, reminiscent of the replicants in Ridley Scott's *Blade Runner*, who are androids fitted with manufactured recollections of childhoods they never had. Forget the deep consciousness of early-twentieth-century thinkers like Freud and Jung, who described a precious and mysterious Self that many still cling to today: training mavens like Macedonia and Stapleton favor a more contemporary, cognitive approach, one that sees consciousness as a result of complex, but ultimately tweakable, informatic systems. And indeed, the idea of the brain as a kind of reprogrammable computer—a philosophical conceit that stretches back at least as far as Norbert Weiner's cybernetic theory of the mid-twentieth century—provides the operative metaphor behind Macedonia's spiel. In that thumbnail vision of how the mind works is also a desire, a hope, that technology could create a form of education that direct, and that powerful, and that certain. In an era of mood-altering drugs and genetic exploration, it would seem like a perfectly rational notion.

The ultimate goal of simulation training, as Macedonia sees it, would be to create these perfect, false memories, manufactured moments of déjà vu that would help the soldiers of the future. The need to train through battle would be lessened, because—not unlike Orson Scott Card's Ender—they would have been fighting near-real virtual battles for years. Macedonia likes to illustrate this by recounting a scene from one of his favorite films, *Patton.*

In what Macedonia sees as the film's greatest scene, the general, en route to the battlefield, tells his driver to turn right. The driver says that's the wrong way. "Don't argue," George C. Scott commands, "I can smell a battlefield." Arriving at an empty spot, Patton makes a cryptic speech. "The battlefield was here," says Scott. "The Carthaginians defending the city were attacked by three Roman legions. They were brave, but they couldn't hold. They were massacred. Arab women stripped them of their tunics and their swords and lances. The soldiers lay naked in the sun, years ago. I was here." Macedonia recites these lines almost verbatim; he says he has seen the film "a thousand times over."

"We have a term in virtual reality research we call presence," Macedonia explains. It is a term describing a kind of ineffable sense of reality—not necessarily produced through visual fidelity, but from a gut feeling of *being there.* "You ever go to a foreign country and you get that sort of creepy feeling? Like, I'm in a different place, I know where I am but . . . ? When Patton gave that speech, I got that sort of creepy feeling. Because what he was saying is, I know about this battle. He says, I was here. I fought this battle, I studied this battle. I know all about this. I read it in Latin, the stories of that battle.

"The thing is," Macedonia continues, "that's what we're trying to do with these soldiers with these training systems. When they go out there, they'll think, I was here. I've been here before. I know what I'm supposed to do. And that's the essence of it."

A cynic might say that Macedonia has a rather lofty metaphysical vision to describe training systems that teach soldiers to fire laser rifles at computer-generated Iraqis, or instruct them how to repair the engine of a Humvee. But that kind of rote response is not what he's talking about. It's about instilling patterns of actions, and making those patterns second nature. Anyone who has played video games for days on end can feel this happening—how not just button-moves and territory maps become internalized, but tactics, approaches, ways of thinking about a crisis.

Call it brain-hacking, or, the triumph of empiricism: all the inchoate, mysterious processes that ebb and flow within subjective experience can and should be understood as purely objective systems, mere nervous mechanics, and once understood, rebuilt as easily as a new microprocessor, reprogrammed like software. For all its logical gloss, it is a philosophy of mind that resonates with the superficial, gaudy, and cartoonish architecture of Orlando: it is about bringing everything to the surface, bringing everything under control, making everything familiar. Like the chain-mall architecture of central Florida, nothing will remain foreign, nothing new; everything will be known. It a perhaps unforeseen end product of cybernetic theory of the 1960s, the same urge that drove the early utopian hackers at MIT and Stanford. The mind is one of the last American frontiers, and military thinkers are eager to scout out and claim a territory that the world of entertainment had almost stumbled upon. We've moved from geological frontiers to virtual ones. All that is complicated and messy will someday be made clean, orderly, and new. A brand-new super-sized subdivision where there once was nothing but swamp—or desert.

Targeting Terrorists

Macedonia's arguments notwithstanding, fun does seem to have its place in military simulation training, at least judging from some of the players at I/ITSEC.

Specialist Samuel England, a fresh-faced nineteen-year-old stationed at the National Training Center in Fort Irwin, California, came to the conference to showcase the Engagement

Skills Trainer 2000, along with a handful of other servicemen and women who came to demonstrate the technology for attendees. England also appears in the EST 2000's video as an actor. Produced by Cubic Defense Applications for PEO STRI, the EST 2000 looks like a simpler, more portable version of the VirTra Systems trainer. It consists of a small theatrical staging area, here decorated with a little scrub and rubble for effect, and a single flat-screen projection that runs interactive movies meant to train for "shoot / don't shoot" decision-making, marksmanship, and collective squad tactics. In one of EST 2000's scenarios, a truck full of Arab male POWs drives through the desert, and then stops for a moment. A few of the prisoners suddenly grab guns and start shooting toward the screen—that is, toward the squad of trainees facing the screen. England and his fellow soldiers shoot back with realistic-looking light-gun rifles. Each accurate hit registers as a tiny, bright red dot.

"Making it was actually pretty fun, just like, I guess, any sort of Hollywood-style thing," England says, grinning. At I/ITSEC, he and two other fellow soldiers shot at the EST 2000 video screen with mock rifles, trying to take down images of actors playing Iraqi insurgents. England explains that "the Iraqis are actually paid people from Titan," a major military contracting firm. "They actually get Iraqi civilians, ex-Iraqi police, and Iraqi military, and they move over to the States. They act in the films, and they work at NTC." (Although Titan reps were unavailable to confirm England's statement, representatives at the National

Training Center said that if such a video were produced at NTC, then their on-site Iraqi employees would likely be involved.)

At the display for *America's Army*—the highly publicized, globally popular online game developed as an Army recruitment tool—local teenagers scrambled to play with the *America's Army* Vehicle Convoy Trainer, which looks like an armed, wheelless Humvee placed in front of an oversized video game screen, depicting yet another virtual Iraq filled with digital insurgents. Though *America's Army* was originally developed as a recruitment aid, it was now being retooled into a training device as well, not only for the military, but also potentially for other agencies like the Secret Service. This means that, when implemented, a gamer could go from playing *America's Army* at home, to signing up for the Army, and then train on the same familiar gaming platform. The game might have been "creating memories" for him long before he had even decided to sign up.

"Fun is central," says Colonel Casey Wardynski, originator and director of the *America's Army* project who has become a familiar figure in the gaming world with *America's Army*'s success. "A 'fun' training system means keeping soldiers engaged voluntarily. This situation makes for better training, and can even extend the training day into the barracks where soldiers could continue to train in their off-time."

Already, the game's official site, AmericasArmy.com, touts that two of the game's development teams, America's Army: Government Applications and America's Army: Future Applications, will feed tidbits of new innovations back onto the free game, to whet the appetites of its devoted online following. Preliminary materials tout the product as a good "return on investment" for a game that initially cost $7.5 million to develop. "The country is at war and to the extent that *America's Army* can play a larger role it should," Wardynski stated in a post-I/ITSEC e-mail interview. "For example, *America's Army* incorporates a fairly extensive set of game missions in which players learn and demonstrate their understanding of the ABCs of lifesaving. In the game, successful completion of these scenarios qualifies a player to serve as a medic. In real life, these missions convey baseline lifesaving skills that anyone who is a first responder could use to save a life. By putting this content into the game, players of *America's Army* can obtain lifesaving skills to address trauma ranging from an accident to untoward terrorist activity."

"We know there is no silver bullet for homeland security," Wardynski writes. "In this case *America's Army* can serve two purposes for one taxpayer investment—communicate with young adults about soldiering and provide Americans with skills to address immediate consequences in a first responder situation." So instead of wasting time battling demons and aliens, kids might learn CPR for fun.

According to Wardynski, the drive to expand *America's Army* came from requests from within different branches of defense and intelligence. "The decision to repurpose elements of the public version of *America's Army* was really demand-driven,"

Wardynski says. "Last year, the U.S. Secret Service expressed interest in working with *America's Army* to improved virtual training afforded to their agents. Since that time we have delivered a variety of assets to the Secret Service for their virtual training environments. At the same time, agencies within the Army approached our team about using the game for a range of applications from cultural awareness and adaptive leadership training to virtual weapons system prototyping and training embedded in new weapons systems."

Wardynski cites several reasons why other organizations were looking to take on their own versions of *America's Army* for training. First, he says, *America's Army* is realistic and engaging. "This makes training fun," he says. The games team playing style is perfect for mission rehearsal. Most importantly, unlike trainers like the EST 2000, which rely on recorded scenarios, *America's Army* can be used as a "virtual classroom," allowing players to practice responses to "new enemy tactics, techniques or procedures" inside the game, using their soldier avatars: in effect, a cheaper, more engaging SIMNET. "This can greatly reduce training costs, development risk, increase frequency of game updates and allow the game to be highly adaptive to human behavior since humans are driving the virtual interactions rather than relatively inflexible AI scripts," he says. *America's Army*, then, could transform from a flashy recruitment tool into a kind of Sim National Training Center.

"It has the ability to overcome the limitations of the physical world," Wardynski says. "In the game environment, you can place a trainee in an infinite variety of situations from their physical setting, to weather and light conditions, level of complexity, level of chaos and then you can replay their performance or alter training conditions."

The fusion of playtime with wartime seems perfectly natural to some of the folks at I/ITSEC. Many of the participating companies play both side of the fence, to some extent: VirTra Systems makes both immersive training devices and theme park attractions, though the former have overtaken the latter in the past four years. "Education, entertainment, training—they're all the same thing," argues Stapleton. "They're all in the same business of making memories for a lifetime. When you get down to that, it's not really about the technology as much as—even though it gives us more capabilities—it's about the impact it has on us."

Hooah for Hollywood

On the other side of the continent lies Marina Del Rey, a little seaside corner of Los Angeles County area that, like Orlando, has begun replacing its outlying, unkempt natural landscape with rows of boxy new condominiums, clustered between the shore and the highway. It's best known for its man-made, 6,000-slip recreational boat harbor—reportedly the world's largest—and the headquarters of ICANN, the nonprofit organization that roughly approximates a governing body for the Internet. During the dot-com boom, Marina Del Rey was home to numerous, now-defunct high-tech start-ups, but another generation of new media has already moved in. Above the palm trees lining Lincoln Boulevard looms a corner-straddling, glass-curtain office box emblazoned with a red "EA" on its side, gleaming in the sun: it's the SoCal satellite of Electronic Arts, the northern California–based video game-publishing titan whose fortunes continue to ride high on the success of franchises like *EA Sports*, *The Lord of the Rings*, *Harry Potter*, *The Sims*, and *SSX*—as well as war-themed series like *Battlefield*, *Medal of Honor,* and *Command and Conquer.* With annual sales exceeding $3 million, EA remains the biggest video game publisher in the world. Millions of people know their slogan, which can be heard, voiced in an awed whisper of a child, as their logo appears before the beginning of one of their products: *EA Games. Challenge Everything.*

Just down the road from EA is another anonymous, squarish office building, with dark blue windows set inside thin columns of concrete white. At its top sits a rather small sign, with a less recognizable logo: the letters *i c t,* lowercased, italicized, and red. A pedestrian-level placard at its base displays the tenant's full name: The Institute for Creative Technologies. In a city dominated by an entertainment industry that's currently lurching into a brave new world of digital culture on multiple fronts, its name could indicate many things: an animation studio, an academic research center, a video game developer, perhaps a special-effects house. In fact, it is indeed a combination of all those things—add to that list military think tank—and it owes its existence to an unprecedented collaboration among Hollywood, Silicon Valley, and the Pentagon.

In October 1996, the National Research Council hosted an exploratory conference about fifty miles south of LA, in Irvine, California. The topic, "Modeling and Simulation: Linking Entertainment and Defense" was the suggestion of Michael Zyda, a polymathic, visionary teacher at the Naval Postgraduate School, who would eventually oversee the development of *America's Army* at the school's MOVES Institute. Zyda perceived that the military, the entertainment industry, and digital technology were all quickly changing, and their point of convergence could be found in simulation. The creation of convincing, make-believe worlds connected Hollywood special effects, the new generation of ever more visually complex video games, and the elaborate multimedia theatrics of theme parks to military interest in simulation training and virtual interfaces for remote warfare.

Videogames were becoming increasingly cinematic, with ever more realistic graphics, Hollywood actors providing voices for characters, and production budgets reaching into the millions. Movies, conversely, were evolving into gamelike spectacles, boasting extended digitally enhanced landscapes, effects, and characters. Since Pixar's *Toy Story*, computer-generated animation was quickly squeezing out its hand-drawn predecessor.

That such an unprecedented powwow was initiated from the military side is significant. During the tail end of the Cold War, the

Reagan policy involved pouring massive amounts of money into defense spending, effectively bankrupting the Soviet Union through an increasingly expensive arms race. As a result, the U.S. military of the 1980s led the world in many technological fields, including computer graphics and simulation training: at a time most civilians had never even heard of the Internet, SIMNET was the most advanced multiuser virtual environment around. But in the 1990s, when Pentagon budgets constricted and the commercial computer and video game industries boomed, suddenly the military found its simulation technology losing ground to Lucasfilm, Sony, and Nintendo. "We'd show our stuff to generals," Zyda told the *New York Times* in 2004, "and they'd say, 'Well, my son is playing something that looks better than that, and it only cost $50.' "

Zyda's conference was a convergence of some very different worlds. In one camp were the military thinkers, from DARPA, the National Guard, the Defense Modeling and Simulation Office, the Office of the Secretary of Defense, the Army, Navy, and Air Force. They collaborated in workshops with representatives from Disney, Pixar, Paramount, George Lucas' Industrial Light & Magic, virtual reality theme park attraction designers Illusion, Inc., video game developers Spectrum Holobyte, and Internet content providers Total Entertainment Network. SIMNET visionary Jack Thorpe rubbed shoulders with Alexander Singer, an award-winning producer-director who worked on *Star Trek: Deep Space 9*, *Star Trek: Voyager,* and many other hit television series.

The conference was thus as much social experiment as it was fact-finding mission, and its participants considered it a great success, even if some of them approached with initial skepticism. "You know, the Hollywood people were like, work with the military? I'm not so sure. And the military people were like, work with the Hollywood folks? Not so sure," says Diane Piepol, an ICT creative director whose computer graphics background includes visual effects for features like *True Lies*, *Speed*, and *Super Mario Brothers*. "But get everyone in the same room, and everyone walked out with their stereotypes destroyed."

In their resulting report, published by the National Research Council, Zyda's committee suggests that "though the two communities differ widely in their structures, incentives, and motivations, opportunities may exist for the entertainment industry and the defense modeling and simulation community to work together to advance the state of the art. . . . By sharing research results, coordinating research agendas, and working collaboratively when necessary, the entertainment industry and the DOD may be able to more efficiently and effectively build a technological base for modeling and simulation that will improve the nation's security and economic performance." The report predicts that defense and entertainment could potentially find mutual benefit toward the research and development of four specific goals: photo-realistic, immersive worlds; multiuser networked environments; standards for interoperability between different systems; and convincingly "intelligent" computer-generated characters.

In just under two hundred pages, *Modeling and Simulation* is relatively brief (that is, as government reports go) but comprehensive in its arguments. Even given its cool, semibureaucratic tone, the writing can't help but exude a bit of dot-com era upbeatness as it catalogs the vast technological possibilities at hand. And the ideas do seem exciting and innovative: it is undoubtedly the only government publication in history to include a serious investigation of the merits of Walt Disney World's *Aladdin* ride, video games *Doom* and *Command and Conquer*, movies like *Forrest Gump* and *Disclosure*, and even Neal Stephenson's science fiction novel *Snowcrash* in order to illustrate challenges to national defense.

Research Areas of Interest to the Entertainment Industry and the Defense Modeling and Simulation Community

Technologies for Immersion

- Image generation—graphics computers capable of generating complex visual images.
- Tracking—technologies for monitoring the head position and orientation of participants in virtual environments.
- Perambulation—technologies that allow participants to walk through virtual environments while experiencing hills, bumps, obstructions, etc.
- Virtual presence—technologies for providing a wide range of sensory stimuli: visual, auditory, olfactory, vibrotactile, and electrotactile.

Networked Simulation

- *Higher-bandwidth networks*—to allow faster communication of greater amounts of information among participants.
- *Multicast and area-of-interest managers*—to facilitate many-to-many communications while using limited bandwidth.
- *Latency reduction*—techniques for reducing true or perceived delays in distributed simulations.

Standards for Interoperability

- *Virtual reality transfer protocol*—to facilitate large-scale networking of distributed virtual environments.
- *Architecture for interoperability*—network and software architectures to allow scalability of distributed simulations without degrading performance.
- *Interoperability standards*—protocols that allow simulators to work together effectively and facilitate the construction of large simulations from existing subsystems.

Computer-Generated Characters

- *Adaptability*—development of computer-generated characters that can modify their behavior automatically over time.
- Individual behaviors—computer-generated characters that accurately portray the actions and responses of individual participants in a simulation rather than those of aggregated entities such as tank crews or platoons.

- *Human representations*–authentic avatars that look, move, and speak like humans.
- *Aggregation/disaggregation*–the capability to aggregate smaller units into larger ones and to disaggregate them back into smaller ones without sacrificing the fidelity of a simulation or frustrating attempts at interoperability.
- *Spectator roles*–ways of allowing observers to watch a simulation.

Tools for Creating Simulated Environments
- *Database generation and manipulation*–tools for managing and storing information in large databases, to allow rapid retrieval of information, feature extraction, creation, and simplification.
- *Compositing*–hardware and software packages that allow designers to combine images taken from different sources (whether live-action footage or three-dimensional models) and to facilitate the addition or modification of lighting and environmental effects.
- *Interactive tools*–hardware and software systems that allow designers to use a variety of input devices (more than mouse and keyboard) to construct models and simulations.

Source: *Modeling and Simulation: Linking Entertainment and Defense*, National Academies Press, 1997, pp. 2-3.

The report also stresses the need for involvement by academia, saying that both the Pentagon and the entertainment industry will need to "foster the establishment and expansion of education programs to train students in the technical and non-technical underpinnings of modeling, simulation, and virtual environments." Such an academic base, the report offers, "not only will produce these students but will also generate many of the technical advances upon which future entertainment and defense systems will be built."

With this in mind, Zyda spent half a year drafting a proposal for the Institute for Creative Technologies, which was subsequently created at the University of Southern California in 1999 with an initial $45 million five-year investment from the Army. The Army saw USC as an ideal partner for a number of reasons: it is home to one of the world's top film schools, enjoys an obvious proximity to major players in the entertainment industry, and like many large universities has a long history of defense-funded research. (The *Modeling and Simulation* report also led to the creation of the Naval Postgraduate School's MOVES Institute in 2000, where the *America's Army* project was developed.) The Army appears to think that ICT has been a successful venture: in 2004, the Army renewed its support more than twofold, this time with a $100 million grant.

The initial personnel lineup for ICT drew from the same intersection of Hollywood, the gaming industry, academia, and the military that had marked Zyda's NRC conference. The staff's resulting eclecticism is worthy of a reality television show. Some of the most well-known names include Randall Kleiser, a USC film school alum and director of pop-camp classics like *Grease*, *Blue Lagoon*, and *Big Top Pee-Wee*; John Milius, director of such grim eighties fantasies as *Red Dawn* and *Conan the Barbarian*, whose screenwriting credits include *Apocalypse Now* and *Clear and Present Danger*; several members of the Sims support team, just as that franchise was beginning to gain a mainstream following; and Ron Cobb, production designer on films like *Star Wars*, *Back to the Future*, and *Alien*. Executive vice president of Paramount Television Group Richard Lindheim was drafted as ICT's executive director.

Even the institute's interior bespeaks a pop culture pedigree: it was crafted by Herman Zimmerman, the production designer of seven *Star Trek* films and three of the franchise's TV series. Jack Valenti, decorated WWII veteran and then notorious president of the Motion Picture Association of American, spoke at ICT's opening dedication and press conference. "Los Angeles is not the 'entertainment capital of the world,' " Valenti joked to the mixed gathering, "Washington, D.C., is the entertainment capital of the world."

Thinking Like Terrorists

The institute made headlines a month after September 11 when *Variety* reported that ICT had hosted a series of meetings between intelligence officials and Hollywood screenwriters and directors (FEDS SEEK H'WOOD'S HELP, the original story declared). The Tinseltown creative types were there to brainstorm possible future terrorist scenarios, drawing on their vast experience crafting blockbuster scripts. The talent pool was a mix of high and low art: brutalist David Fincher (*Fight Club*, *Se7en*), erstwhile music video and skateboard-tape director Spike Jonze (*Being John Malkovich*), ICT creative consultant Randall Kleiser, the screenwriters of *The Rocketeer*, and a bevy of action specialists: *Die Hard*'s screenwriter, *MacGyver's* TV scriptwriter, and director Joseph Zito, the helmer of such flicks as *Delta Force One*, *Missing in Action*, *Invasion USA*, and *Friday the 13th: The Final Chapter*.

With the nation still nerve-racked from the East Coast attacks, the item was picked up by papers nationwide, prompting both anxious commentary about the encroachment of a new militarized America into the heart of pop culture, and skepticism that Hollywood dream merchants would have anything to offer toward something as serious as the War on Terror. A few days later, *Variety*'s editor in chief, Peter Bart, weighed in on the reaction. "This war may go on sporadically for years," he wrote. "If that's the case, the key players better find a way to sustain audience involvement." But he ended on a more congratulatory, if cynical, note: "Let's applaud the writers and directors for giving it a try. They're accustomed to brainstorming on demand. . . . Now they face a new cast of characters: self-styled holy men who finance their operations peddling heroin; weirdos slipping anthrax into newsrooms; nihilists who've been brainwashed into thinking they have a ticket to paradise. On reflection, all this may be too surreal even for Hollywood."

The attacks on New York and Washington did seem like scenes from Hollywood blockbusters: in a devastatingly unwelcome way, life appeared to imitate art. In trying to process something deeply unfamiliar and nightmarish, Americans—and observers worldwide—fell back on the imaginary versions of destruction our minds knew best. "The blockbuster's lingua franca is violent action," New York film critic J. Hoberman observed a few weeks after the attacks. "Thus, the déjà vu of crowds fleeing *Godzilla* through Lower Manhattan canyons, the wondrously exploding skyscrapers and bellicose rhetoric of *Independence Day*, the romantic pathos of *Titanic*, the wounded innocence of *Pearl Harbor*, the cosmic insanity of *Deep Impact.*" If such was the case, who better to predict what might happen next than the blockbuster creators themselves?

That first conference sparked an ongoing project at ICT with the CIA, reports Catherine Kominos, director of administration at ICT and former deputy director of research at the Pentagon. The current effort consists of three-day workshops with directors and writers "just coming up with scenarios for issues they're looking at. Brainstorming sessions, basically, about plausible stories. It's mostly for training. They find it very valuable." The CIA, she explains, is "trained in a certain way; there's not much out-of-the-box thinking. So this helps them."

The Next Generation

The interior of ICT feels creative-corporate; it could be the digs of an animation studio or advertising agency. Surfaces are sleek and rounded, everywhere covered in blond wood; even the ceiling curves like the roof of a Parisian arcade. The circular, multitiered coffee-break nook looks like it might take off into orbit. Large glass windows look out onto repetitive rows of new condos. Many of the offices are designed with built-in beds. Near the elevators are small lobbies; copies of the *Hollywood Reporter* and *Variety* lie beneath screens that display ICT promo videos, filled with digitally rendered soldiers and men working at computer terminals. On one floor there's a modest-sized, tiered amphitheater with canvas-covered seats augmented by stacks of colorful pillows. There's brain worker clutter here and there: a SIGGRAPH presentation mounted on foamcore lies in the corner of a hallway. An old strategy game from the 1960s called *Twixt* lies out on a table of a common area, partially constructed: it looks like the kind of abstract logic puzzle they would have obsessed over at Rand back in the day.

Affixed to the door to the graphics laboratory with a strip of black gaffer's tape, a sheet of white paper bears a laser-printed message: *"Please do not enter. Rad experiment in progress . . ."* Inside is the workshop of Paul Debevec, ICT's executive producer for graphics research, who's famous in digital-effects circles as the inventor of "bullet time:" the balletic 3-D slow-mo effect that became popularized through the *Matrix* films, and has by now become used so many times, it's become a digital-effects cliché. Debevec is soft-eyed, goateed man in his thirties, sporting a black button-down shirt, tucked into belted khakis. At ICT, he has been investigating ways to replicate within virtual environments the many ways light falls on objects in real life. To this end, he and his team have been working since 2001 to complete the world's most exact virtual replica of Athens' Parthenon, both in its current form and how it would have appeared 2,500 years ago, in all its original glory. Photos and news clippings of the ancient monument are posted around the workshop; in a corner near his office lays a plaster replica of what appears to be a portion of the Elgin Marbles.

An exacting digital re-creation of the Parthenon might seem like a strange goal for an institute primarily funded for the needs of national defense with taxpayer dollars; at the very least, one assumes, the Army will be utterly prepared if we need to occupy the Acropolis. But Debevec sees the choice as prag-matic. "It seemed the most appropriate to keep the team inspired, to be able to bring in interns who would be thrilled to work for free on these kind of things," he says. "It is something that was of international importance and everyone agreed that this was an excellent idea for demonstrating and pushing for-ward a lot of these techniques."

As an elaborate test case, the process of creating a digital Parthenon, ICT believes, will advance 3-D computer graphics toward greater verisimilitude. The government, academia and the entertainment industry, Debevec explains, each have their "own need for photorealistic computer graphics, and also interesting immersive environments, to be used specifically for education, for training and for entertainment." It's a perfect example of the once-accidental defense research inspiring the commercial sector, now planned from the get-go as creative synergy.

While Debevec works in a realm of almost pure research, he's very cognizant of the high-tech tradition in which he operates. "The sponsorship of computer graphics research goes all the way back to the military in the 1940s and the 1950s," he says. "Computer science itself is the result of military funding in World War II to originally calculate mathematical equations. A lot of what is going on with computer graphics was pushed forward with flight simulator research, to create virtual views of an airplane flying over terrain, so the people sitting in a fake version of the airplane cockpit could see what they're supposed to see out there. And as a result of this, those algorithms that were developed in the seventies and the eighties, these are now in the computer graphics cards that you use to play video games with today."

In one corner of the graphics lab sits a ten-foot-tall device that resembles the skeleton of a geodesic dome, with light fixtures set into its black metal framework, pointing inward. It looks like something out of *The Matrix* itself. When an intern steps inside the sphere, Debevec demonstrates how the apparatus is able to replicate specific kinds of light, some of which had actually been recorded on location. It could be arranged, for island nation itself. Japanese game reviews, he found, had barely anything to say about the potentially disturbing fact that Japanese players would be slaughtering characters representing their own countrymen.

"We're accustomed to thinking that a piece of entertainment is nothing but its cultural content," Thompson writes. "A movie or TV show is just what you see on the screen. But a game is also about play, and play is invisible. That's why outsiders are often puzzled by the success of games that would appear to be nothing but screamingly offensive content. They can't see the play. Sure, you've got raw guts flying around—but for the player, part of the joy is in messing with physics (even if that happens to be bullets and shoulder-launched grenades) or with strategy (even if that's figuring out how to starve a village)."

Games are indeed modes of action—activities, not just representations. Yet adding an overarching historical narrative to a game can add a layer of meaning—and uncanniness—that a more fantasy-based game would not have. Given how insistent game companies are in promoting the historical veracity of their war games, it is difficult to play these without some moments of divided consciousness, without thinking about how you are at some level reenacting a historical occurrence. In *Medal of Honor: Rising Sun*, for instance, finishing each level rewards the player with an unlocked movie: black-and-white newsreel documentary footage of the actual event you just played. Playing the earliest chapters of the game, I could not help but think about my grandfather, who had himself fought in the Pacific during WWII, and was a veteran of the attack on Pearl Harbor, the event framing the opening segment of *Rising Sun*. As I maneuvered my way through a sinking warship, perishing multiple times until I found the correct means of escape, I pondered how strange it was that I was reenacting a horrific, soul-altering episode in my grandfather's life, an event that resulted in the deaths of many men he knew, and subsequently plunged the U.S. into the largest war in history. What would he have thought that the attack on Pearl Harbor, six decades later, had become something to kill a little time with on the weekends? (Or that I was in fact participating in a second-form simulation, at least as equally indebted to the imagination of Michael Bay as to the historical record?)

On another occasion, I spent a late afternoon with *Rising Sun* picking off Japanese soldiers in Burma, usually by shooting them in the head with a sniper rifle as they popped up from hidden foxholes, like armed whack-a-moles. After far too much time with my Xbox, I ventured beyond my apartment to attend a screening of Hara Kazuo's *The Emperor's Naked Army Marches On*. A controversial Japanese vérité-style documentary from 1987, Hara's film follows Okuzaki Kenzo, an obsessed and deranged antiwar activist who's on a mission to confront veterans linked to a military execution of two Imperial soldiers in New Guinea at the close of World War II. Hara and Okuzaki barge into the homes of elderly ex-soldiers, where the activist harangues them about their involvement in the affair. Few are forthcoming, though one reveals the incident involved forced cannibalism. The climax of the film involves the interrogation of one particularly frail veteran who served on the execution squad and remains resolutely tight-lipped about the event. Okuzaki suddenly wrestles the old man to the ground, punching him in the face repeatedly as Hara's camera continues to roll. The veteran's wife calls the police, as she calmly insists on "no violence" from her physically demonstrative houseguest.

The juxtaposition of *Medal of Honor: Rising Sun* and *The Emperor's Naked Army Marches On* could not have revealed a starker contrast. Hara's film, shot decades after the event, reveals the war as an invisible, unspeakable trauma, something still churning within the men who fought it forty years earlier. In Hara's film, the events of World War II are never seen, yet they are nevertheless *felt* in a powerful way, like lingering ghosts haunting the souls of the living. *Rising Sun* is filled with representations of the war, but they are just bodies without ghosts, images of hollow CGI puppets, bereft of interior experience, mere targets for my Thompson M1 SMG, M1911 Pistol, or Type 97 Hand Grenade. There are some elements of historical realism that war games aren't capable of—or at least have not yet been designed to achieve.

Thompson is correct in one major regard: if *Rising Sun* were a crappy game, I would not have stayed with it long enough to ponder its existential resonances (note, for example, that I'm not bothering to delve into my experiences with digital lemon *Black Hawk Down*). But this does not mean that its historical meanings are beside the point of the game experience, even if they may be ancillary effects, about which it is difficult to generalize. With gaming companies pushing historical realism, pondering the gap between their increasingly intricate simulations and the lived experience of actual people seems inevitable. Playstations, PCs, and Xboxes are plentiful on American bases in Iraq: how many young servicemen experience those perhaps unsubtle twinges of double vision, as they snipe virtual insurgents inside imaginary Middle Eastern cities? And after all, isn't this creepy, semimorbid disjunction part of the appeal of video games in the first place?

The Sick Factor

The makers of *Kuma\War* argue that their games have an educational, or at least informational value, allowing players a better understanding of how contemporary events have transpired. "We can let you experience the news in ways the networks cannot," Kuma CEO Keith Halper told *Wired* in 2004. By transforming this information into a virtual, explorable space and creating a playable narrative, Kuma claims that it wants to approximate a documentary in game form. The project gives new life to the title of the old historical-dramatization television show *You Are There*.

A similar argument was made by the creators of *JFK Reloaded*, a commercial downloadable simulation of President John F. Kennedy's assassination produced by a Scottish company that debuted on the forty-first anniversary of the event. Its makers claimed that the game was a serious attempt to explore the Warren Commission's "lone gunman" theory: the player's perspective is that of Lee Harvey Oswald's schoolbook depository aerie, looking down to the presidential limousine moving through Dealey Plaza, and the challenge is to kill Kennedy with three bullets in the exact same manner the Warren Commission's report alleges. Each shot is judged on a point scale for how closely it matches the three theoretical trajectories of report; the company offered a cash prize to anyone who scored a perfect 1,000. Naturally, the game spurred controversy. A spokesperson for Senator Ted Kennedy—whose office was no doubt overjoyed to field press queries on the matter—simply called it "despicable."

Reviewing the game for *Slate*, Clive Thompson nearly countered his own argument about the Japanese reception of *Medal of Honor: Rising Sun*; he praised *JFK Reloaded*'s complex ballistics, but found the level of detail too unnerving. "When you peer through the rifle scope, the faces of JFK and Jacqueline Kennedy (and Texas Gov. John Connally and his wife Nellie) are completely recognizable. These are real people who still have immediate living relatives—or, in the case of Nellie Connally, are still alive," he writes. "When I finally managed to kill JFK and watched his head blow open while he flopped forward like a rag doll, I was genuinely horrified. The game wants you to think about what's happening as a mere physics experiment, but you can't, nor would you want to."

Thompson's shift in focus is testament to how moral boundaries for video games currently remain in flux. Gamers galore came to the defense of Rockstar's ultraviolent but brilliant *Grand Theft Auto* series, yet *JFK Reloaded* saw few public apologists. And the makers of *Medal of Honor* and *JFK Reloaded* alike play into this rapid change. For Electronic Arts, their slogan "Real War, Real Games" sells the novelty of being able to play unprecedentedly "real" simulations of famous historical events; in a few years, *Medal of Honor* will look clunky, but for now, it's relatively close to the cutting edge. The makers of *JFK Reloaded* sling some boilerplate hooey about how their game is meant to be educational, knowing full well that links to its site will be forwarded all over the Internet, half in outrage, the rest in prurient curiosity. *JFK Reloaded* perpetrates the old sideshow trick favored by carnies and exploitation filmmakers: serve up something immoral but seductive, then put on airs of mock seriousness as the cash register ka-chings. The huckster's crocodile tears of moral seriousness help get anyone waffling about the sideshow in the door; everyone else confident enough about their own curiosity is heading in anyway.

This "sick factor" goes as far a back as freak shows and old exploitation films like *Faces of Death*, but gained an interactive twist as it entered video games with early first-person shooters like *Wolfenstein 3D* and *Doom*. The sick factor is the cheap thrill of moral naughtiness—the idea that you can do something immoral without repercussion in a virtual world—and anyone who enjoys games knows well this pleasure. It is the *raison d'être of* play-the-criminal games like the *Grand Theft Auto* series and its imitators, and cannot be discounted as part of why war games are so pleasurable. Even more than the practice of war itself, war games release us into a realm where our normal moral compunctions may be discarded: we can kill other people and destroy property. Some games, like *America's Army*, cloak this chance to kill in the formal code of conduct that the real Army theoretically abides by at all times. Other games allow for a more free-for-all experience, to various degrees. If these games were designed with the same level of moral complexity as films like *Saving Private Ryan* or *The Emperor's Naked Army Marches On*—fleshing out your puppet-opponents into more fully realized human adversaries—they might not be so fun.

An Education in War

JFK Reloaded may have been nothing more than a flashy exploitative prank, but others have proposed the concept of investigating history through video games more seriously. The History Channel, for example, produced a two-hour television special in 2005 based on and named after the video game series *Brothers in Arms*: a slam-dunk marketing tie-in, perhaps, but nonetheless a novel way to use the visual historical information the game presents. In the special, historical events of World War

II are replayed in the game, as a kind of low-budget CGI; these were combined with live-action reenactments and historical newsreel footage, often cutting back and forth quickly within the same scene. As a work of history, it is of course still fraught with the same issues of, say, teaching about the Holocaust using a cinematic work of historical fiction like *Schindler's List*.

Some of those few academics who take video games seriously have proposed that games might be capable of more than mere illustration. In his study *More Than a Game: The Computer Game as Fictional Form*, Barry Atkins offers that games can look at history in ways that noninteractive media like movies can't. Atkins argues that the practice of video gaming allows the player to engage in counterfactual narratives: speculations based on those "what if" questions often pondered by science-fiction authors and historians, particularly of the military variety. There are limits to the flexibility of counterfactuals in video games, however: most games have fairly fixed narrative pathways, with the only forking options boiling down to (a) continue or (b) die. "Sandbox" games like *Grand Theft Auto* or massively multiplayer online role-playing games allow for many more decisions, but counterfactual gaming in these instances seems either irrelevant or unremarkable. However, it's entirely likely that more complex historical-narrative games could appear in the future. Some history teachers have already begun to use games like *Civilization*, for example.

Historical counterfactuals figure more prominently as the

premises of certain *Kuma\War* games, which allow the player to explore what might happen if alternate plans for the hunting of Osama bin Laden or the rescue of American hostages in Iran had been carried out. But this kind of counterfactual investigation leans toward the tactical, rather than questioning larger aspects of the development of civilizations beyond the outcome on the battlefield. More sociologically detailed alternative histories remain, for now, the stuff of literature.

MIT media scholar Henry Jenkins has suggested that using war games might even have a usefully cathartic effect. "We use games to work through the intense anxieties surrounding modern warfare, to bring it at least momentarily under our symbolic control," he writes. "This view was widely shared among child psychologists in the World War II era who encouraged kids to enact military conflicts and even sanctioned playing the role of the enemy as a way of feeling more control over their lives." ICT and the Office of Naval Research are pursuing this idea in a more clinical manner: a project is under way to retool *Full Spectrum Warrior* for use in therapy for soldiers with posttraumatic stress disorder. In theory, the game would be used to create "trigger events" like gunfire and explosions as part of a veteran's recuperative process.

The use of war games for serious matters like historical investigation or mental therapy remain specialized, largely speculative enterprises, however. As they are currently designed, historical war games seem little more educational than the toy soldier crazes of the nineteenth century. Men and boys a century ago enjoyed collecting armies of different historical eras and re-creating famous battles with them; toy soldier manufacturers rolled out lines based on the participants of contemporary wars as they were occurring, and noted swifter sales under those circumstances. Young boys and laddish men may have played Cossacks and squaddies as the Crimean War blossomed overseas. While this kind of pursuit might be seen as educational to an extent, it's instructive to recall the words of historian George L. Mosse, who argued that this education was a limited one: "History came alive, but it was history as a military struggle." With video games, it's a particularly short-sighted struggle. None of these games offer representations much beyond the immediate experience of close combat, or at best, stealth operations leading up to the same. The geopolitical ramifications of war, the impact on civilians, the lingering ancillary casualties and long-term psychological effects play no part in video games—not in the least because these aspects of war can't really be made fun.

Consider Kuma's mission number 43, "Abu Ghraib Prison." Players take on the role of Marines tasked with keeping security around the prison during an insurgent attack. Surely there are more complex and pressing historical lessons to be learned from Abu Ghraib than how best to police the actual building, but Kuma's focus on creating action-packed entertainment out of contemporary events does not seem quite up to the task.

Final Fantasies

Videogames have not always attempted such a straightforward depiction of real war. In the 1970s and 1980s—an age of lower resolution—references to real warfare were more obscure. The perfectly even formation marching of the aliens in *Space Invaders* may be seen as a design limitation of its age, but it also evokes fantasies of über-rationalized Nazi storm troopers or Soviet military parades. A 1977 arcade shooter called *M-79 Ambush* may be the earliest attempt to evoke a specific historical conflict through a video game. The game took its title from a type of grenade launcher used during the Vietnam War. Its console came equipped with squat, short-nosed guns built to look like their namesake, and the cabinet was decorated with comic-book explosions and jungle foliage.

More often, references to specific weapons or military vehicles were mixed into a scenario based on science-fiction themes, creating an odd blend of history and fantasy, as if to partially disavow any connections to real war. The most famous example would be 1980's legendary *Missile Command*. Even with its minimalist graphics, the game clearly depicts thermonuclear war, with ICBMs slowly streaking toward vulnerable cities. If a city is hit, it explodes in a little mushroom cloud. *Missile Command* evokes the ultimate Cold War fear, yet its arcade console was printed with cartoons of futuristic winged spaceships, and its marketing included images of *Buck Rogers*-style spacemen at control panels. The 1980 arcade shooter *Tomahawk Missile* pits the player against not Soviets, but flying saucers. This aspect of eighties games could be seen as mere effect of imprecise package design; since graphics capabilities were low, the identities of a game's enemies, protagonists, and setting were augmented by exterior elements like console art, which might present merely a mishmash of stuff young boys might like: laser beams, machine guns, space soldiers. But as graphics became more sophisticated, the blend of reality and fantasy remained. Perhaps the most extreme instance is 1990s arcade game *NAM-1975*, in which an American solider must return to Vietnam in order to stop an evil scientist who has perfected a deadly laser cannon.

Moreover, eighties pop culture frequently projected war into fantasy realms, perhaps influenced by a generation of parents who had seen their peers die in Vietnam. Games like these were to be expected from an era that produced films like *Raiders of the Lost Ark*, with its supernatural Nazis, or the *Star Wars* franchise, which translated WWII naval battles into impossibly swift and noisy outer-space dogfights. While the U.S. was led by a movie-star president, the "real American hero" GI Joe transmuted from camo dress-up doll to action figure, leaving behind the real-world enemies he fought before 1970 in order to search out and destroy fictional terrorist organization COBRA. After all, for the first generation of American video game kids, real wars were something that had happened almost before they were born, even if the prospect of nuclear conflict between the superpowers loomed as an horrific possibility.

This blending of real and unreal began to change with the Gulf War, which brought with it a small but significant output of video games based on U.S. and British involvement in that conflict. Most were straight-up tank and flight simulators, designed to show off the graphics capabilities of a new generation of PCs. In 1991, Spectrum Holobyte released one such PC game, *Tank*, which put players in control of an M1A1 Abrams tank on desert patrol. Its box cover proudly advertised that *Tank* was "based on the US Army's SIMNET." Software publisher Absolute Entertainment followed with their own series of Abrams first-person sims for Nintendo, *Super Battletank: War in the Gulf*, and *Super Battletank 2*, which included skirmishes introduced by a pixelly General Norman Schwarzkopf, while Electronic Arts entered the post–Desert Storm vogue with the popular *M1 Abrams Battletank*. Sega even released a 1994 arcade game developed with assistance from military contractor Lockheed Martin: *Desert Tank*, a higher-res update of Atari's *Battlezone*. The air war likewise provided game-developer fodder: in 1991, Microprose released *F-15 II Operation Desert Storm*, a new scenario for its 1989 title *F-15 Strike Eagle II*, which had presciently included an original Persian Gulf scenario.

Given the speedy conclusion of Operation Desert Storm, Gulf War games had to alter the odds in order to provide a better game challenge—which also jibed with America's favored self-image as go-it-alone rebels. "In a curious reversal of America's Gulf War odds, you got to play the US Armed Forces as underdog," J. C. Herz observes of *Super Battletank*, "It's just you and your 115 millimeter cannon against all of Saddam Hussein's SCUD launchers, mines, helicopters, tanks, and the entire Iraqi army." In other words, it's the Gulf War rewritten with the logic of *Battlezone* or *Space Invaders*.

Other Gulf War games were more low-tech. *Spit on Saddam*, early shareware game for Mac in the black-and-white line graphics of the time, worked like simple interactive propaganda, made to help American computer users get in the Saddam-hating spirit; an informational title screen requests donations to a college fund for dependents of war casualties, to be sent to the game's producers, the Arkansas-based Plaid Software Group. Players earn "expectorant points" (a takeoff on role-playing games' experience points) by shooting down Scud missiles launched from an onion-domed building, and then spend the points on various forms of spit to be splattered on a crude cartoon of Saddam Hussien's face, which appears as the voice of a G. H. W. Bush imitator drawls, "Come on out, Sadd'm." Ten points get a "raspberry," while thirty buy a "lung biscuit," which is unloaded with a hocking sound effect upon point-and-click. Crudely made and jingo-populist, *Spit on Saddam* is its era's digital equivalent to a "This Scud's for You" T-shirt.

A stranger attempt at Gulf War exploitation was *Operation Secret Storm*, produced in 1991 by Color Dreams, an infamously sketchy firm that produced low-budget indie games for the Nintendo Entertainment System. Opening with cartoon images of

Saddam Hussein surrounded by robed guards, and then a child-like map of Iraq (titled in cute bubble lettering), *Operation Secret Storm* is little more than a clumsy Mario rip-off. The mustachioed plumber has been replaced by a karate-kicking American operative, who must fight storybook Arabs, bald eagles, armed female soldiers, and eventually Hussein himself, amid a multitiered landscape of oil barrels and palm trees. According to Color Dreams programmer John Valesh, the game was originally titled *Who's Sane Now* and was supposed to have been released during the war, but was delayed. The "official reason," Valesh claims, was that Color Dreams staffers were afraid that "Saddam Hussein may try to kill us." The firm had better luck with its more lucrative Christian titles for Nintendo like *Spiritual Warfare* and *Bible Adventures*, released through its Wisdom Tree subsidiary.

Foreign Bodies

A notable limitation of these games, from *Operation Secret Storm* to *SOCOM Navy Seals,* is that their depictions of war present almost exclusively an American—or occasionally British—perspective. In this regard, they mirror the conventions of Hollywood cinema and television, who typically find some way to frame global events from an American point of view, thinking that domestic audiences won't identify with a foreign protagonist.

There have been commercial games that have allowed for

non-Anglo-American participation in historical conflicts. In hobby war gaming, playing "enemy" sides of historical battles is common, and this aspect appears in some of the more computer war games catering to this crowd. Some World War II PC strategy titles like Atomic Game's 1997 *Close Combat II: A Bridge Too Far* allowed players to fight on the German side; Sega's 1994 *Panzer General* caused some controversy due to the fact that you could *only* play a Nazi general (later versions allowed a choice between Allied or Axis perspectives).

Or consider the case *Battlefield 1942,* which enjoyed a following far beyond the traditional war gaming hobbyist scene. The original game, released in 2002, is set in World War II, and is popular as a multiplayer online game, in which players can take on roles within the numerous Axis or Allied forces and fight battles based loosely on real events. *Desert Combat*, a free mod created by the U.S.-based Trauma Studios, changes the setting to Iraq during Operation Desert Storm. By far the most successful *Battlefield 1942* mod, *Desert Combat* became particularly popular after the U.S. invasion of Iraq in 2003. While American gamers played as American forces, German gamers often choose to play Iraqi forces. During a time when many Germans strongly opposed the U.S. invasion, an international debate on foreign policy was being symbolically slogged out inside a virtual Iraq.

Other games appeared from designers outside the U.S. offering an explicitly Arab perspective: the Lebanese *Special*

Force and a pair of games from Syria, *Under Ash* and its sequel, *UnderSiege*. Like the post-9/11 spate of American war-themed video games, these Middle Eastern games portray specific historical conflicts, but do so from radically different points of view. Their very existence is predicated as a riposte to an American-based game culture that disavows the biases of its own game content.

In *Under Ash*, produced by Damascus-based game publisher Dar El Fikr, the protagonist is Ahmad, a Palestinian teenager growing up under Israeli occupation during the first Intifada. In the game's opening chapter, Ahmad runs through his village, throwing stones at Israeli soldiers. Later in the game, Ahmad moves from stones to guns, and shoots at Israeli settlers attempting to push out the Palestinian villagers. In a dramatic trailer for *Under Ash*, a bulldozer destroys a Palestinian home, and Israeli police stomp and kick a Palestinian villager. Ahmad throws a stone into a black void; it transforms into a grenade in midair.

The designers of *Under Ash* state their goals explicitly on the game's Web site, citing the lack of video games that allow for a non-American perspective. "The main purpose of the game was originally filling the time of leisure which this section feels and previously filled with foreign games distorting the facts and history and planting the motto of 'Sovereignty is for power and violence according to the American style.'" Dar El Fikr designer Radwan Qasmiyya says that the game allows Arabs to support the Palestianian cause, albeit in a virtual manner. "The Arab street is very charged. They believe they can't do anything to help their brothers in Palestine," he told BBC News in 2002. "So I think they are playing because they feel that they can feel the experience of young Palestinian people living in Jerusalem." ("Like the game," the BBC reporter concludes ruefully, "the nature of Arab support is largely virtual.")

The game's more elaborate sequel, *UnderSiege*, is set during the second Intifada, between 1999 and 2002. Its narrative draws from true events experienced by Palestinian families during this time; its publisher, Afkarmedia, hopes to release it world-wide. "I just can't wait for *UnderSiege* to be published interna-tionally," Qasmiyya told an interviewer for Selectparks' blog, "so players can tell the difference between a history game based on lives of real people trying to survive ethnic cleansing and a political propaganda that is trying to inject morals in future marines to justify their assaults on nations far away from their homeland." Short teaser videos for *UnderSiege* have the air of a brutal documentary. In one, after a child is gunned down in the street, an Israeli soldier jumps from his tank, apparently to rescue him. When he arrives by his side, he appears to finish him off by pounding him with a cement block. In another teaser, a Palestinian religious service is interrupted by an Orthodox Jewish gunman, who mows down the congregation with a machine gun. The latter scenario appears to depict the 1994 attack on a Hebron mosque by Baruch Goldstein, which killed twenty-nine and has historical distinction as the bloodiest attack on Palestinians by a lone Jewish extremist.

Special Force, published by the Hizbollah Central Internet Bureau in 2003, is based on the guerrilla battles waged against Israel during its occupation of South Lebanon, which ended in 2000. Created from the Genesis 3D open-source game engine, its name perhaps unwittingly parallels *America's Army: Special Forces*, released the same year. Its makers say they intend the game to be "educational for our future generations and for all freedom lovers." In the game, players train at a Lebanese war college, firing guns and lobbing grenades at images of Prime Minster Ariel Sharon and other Israeli leaders, and are awarded medals from real-life Hizbollah secretary general Hassan Nas-rallah upon completion. When battling Israeli forces in South Lebanon, players can honor photos of actual "martyrs" at spots of their real-life death. Israeli bad guys shout, "You killed me" in Hebrew when felled. Moments in the game are decorated by Hizbollah's insignia, or a blue Star of David with a hissing snake at its center.

"The military posts that are attacked in the game by the player are the exact replicas of the posts used by the 'Israelis' during their brutal occupation," the *Special Force* Web site reads. "In the game the player has to attack the military post and liberate it as the Lebanese actually did. The player attacks military personal and not civilians; the attack also takes place on Lebanese soil. In the game you will also find pictures of all the martyrs that died during their struggle to liberate their land so that our children may live in freedom . . . *Special Force* game will render you a partner of the resistance."

A March 2003 Reuters item reported that *Special Force* was advertised on Lebanese television and promoted by one Internet café operator by decorating his business with plastic rifles and sandbags because "guys like that stuff" (a tactic not too far removed from the guns-n-camo militaristic displays decorating American game boutiques around the same time). "The goal is to create an alternative to similar Western games where Arabs and Muslims are portrayed as terrorists," Hizbollah spokesman Bilal at-Zein told the reporter, while an eight-year-old interviewee said he liked *Special Force* "because it kills Israelis . . . I can be a resistance fighter, even though in real life I don't want to do that."

China has also produced its own nationalist game. Set in World War II, *Anti-Japan War Online* is a massively multiplayer online game designed by Chinese firm PowerNet Technology in collaboration with the China Communist Youth League (CCYL) in 2005. The game allows players to participate in battles waged during the Japanese invasion of China from 1937 to 1945, but only from the Chinese side; the war fighting itself is presented in miniature, its sponsors say, to minimize violence. CCYL official Chen Xiao told news agency Interfax that *Anti-Japan War Online* is "a patriotic online game that is both interesting and instructive, and can attract and guide young players," created in response to the dearth of games that conveyed a "national

spirit." Chen states that the Youth League "will pay close attention to the authenticity of historical facts in the game." Interfax
adds that CCYL has already begun projects with other firms:
with Guangdong Data Communication Network, the youth
group is developing Guohun Online (National Spirit Online),
budgeted at more than six million dollars, while with Beijing
Magical Digit Company, CCYL plans three other games: *Sim
Battle: Blue Helmet China*, *Sim Battle: Sky Dragon*, and *Sim
Battle: Long March*, the last title presumably based on brutal
military campaigns led by Mao Zedong against the Kuomintang
in the 1930s, celebrated for over half a century by the Chinese
Communist Party.

Anti-Japan War Online isn't the only Asian analog to American war video games, though it promises to be the most accom-
plished. Right after September 11th, the Taiwanese company
INSREA hastily updated a Korean title called *X-Tank* by adding
a desert environment to the game and retitling it *Final Battle
Afghanistan X-Tank*, complete with a photo of Osama Bin Laden
serving as its box-cover art. "We're the first company to make
software for a game specifically themed on the conflict in
Afghanistan," INSREA's marketing director, Hu Long-yun, proudly
told the *Taipei Times* in early 2002, adding "We wish Bin Laden
would contact us so we could give him a copy of the game." (The
Taipei Times, however, reports that *Final Battle Afghanistan X-
Tank*'s "graphics are dull, the action sleep-inducing and the
Afghan map unconvincing.")

Around the same time, a toy company in Guangzhou, China, called Panyu Gaoming Electronic churned out a cheaply made LCD handheld game called *Laden vs USA*. Its overwrought packaging is decorated with photos of airplanes slamming into the World Trade Center, the subsequent wreckage, and the faces of Bin Laden and a scowling Bush, all mashed up into an overwrought digital collage in imitation of a Hollywood blockbuster advertisement. The game is recommended for "Ages 5 and Up" and seems to have nothing to do with the 9/11 attacks or the war in Afghanistan. The initial levels of the game involve shooting down airplanes and boats with a submarine, depicted with barely discernible graphics using a technology almost two decades old. Upon completion of a level, *Laden vs USA* plays a pinging version of the Christmas carol "Deck the Halls."

As a slapdash product, quickly shipped out from China's seemingly endless trinket and geegaw factories, *Laden vs USA* is a video game example of the strangely off-key 9/11 memorabilia that could be found in any American Chinatown emporia within the first few weeks of the event: items like cigarette lighters that seemed to spark flames off the top of the burning towers or added blinking lights to the points of impact, World Trade Center snow globes emblazoned with the slightly inappropriate slogan "Don't Forget," or DVD compilations of 9/11 news footage designed to look like action-packed Hollywood epics. These souvenirs offer a strange blend of crass commercial opportunism and misguided cultural translation; they're the kind of poorly thought-out commodities that the U.S. once shilled to other nations. J. Hoberman's observation about Chinese 9/11 DVDs with titles like *The Century's Great Catastrophe, Surprise Attack on America* and *America's Disaster: The Pearl Harbor of the 21st Century* rings true as well for *Laden vs USA* and its sense of cross-cultural disjunction: "Suddenly, the Chinese were us—enjoying the spectacle of cataclysmic mass destruction from a safe vantage point. Cool!"

POV Shots

While *Laden vs USA* and *Final Battle Afghanistan X-Tank* provide interesting examples of non-American attempts to cash in on contemporary conflicts, the overtly political agendas espoused by the makers of *Special Force* and *Under Ash* merit closer attention. Artist and academic Alexander R. Galloway— one of a younger generation of scholars who have recently taken to reading video games as forms of culture—offers a provocative reading of these pro-Arab games, contrasting them with mainstream U.S. games like *America's Army.* He suggests that *Under Ash* and *Special Force* explore the potential for a more complex form of realism in gaming, one closer to a concept of "social realism" that Galloway draws from older art forms like Italian neorealist postwar cinema, the literature of Flaubert, and the painting of Courbet. Social realist artworks, in Galloway's definition, "reflect critically on the minutia of everyday life, replete as it is with struggle, personal drama and injustice"; they provide models of realism based on socially-aware narratives, not mere visual fidelity.

By this standard, he argues, *Under Ash* and *Special Force* achieve greater realism than *America's Army*, even though the latter game is of a higher technical caliber. The average player of *America's Army* does not live the globetrotting military existence depictued in that game, but "players of *Under Ash*," Galloway writes, "have a personal investment in the struggle depicted in the game, just as they have a personal investment in the struggle happening each day around them." And since Galloway's notion of social realism requires that a game provide resonance with the player's own everyday life, the effects depend on the specific interaction between gamer and game: the actions he or she performs in the game must speak to the greater reality around them. "To put it bluntly, a typical American youth playing *Special Force* is most likely not experiencing realism," Galloway says, "where as realism is indeed possible for a young Palestinian gamer playing *Special Force* in the occupied territories. This fidelity of context is key for realism in gaming."

The kind of cultural solipsism that Galloway describes rings true for gaming, in ways that it does not with these other art forms. Many video games are based around conflict, and first-person shooters especially are structured around an "us" and "them" far more rigidly divided than most novels or films. Games don't do much in the way of conveying the interior experiences of one's comrades or opponents: these forces appear as merely puppet bodies that give aid or deal ill. The single interior experience that takes place is in the mind of the person playing: therefore, military games with real-world themes tend to "play to" the ideological predilections of the gamer. Thus an American playing a game like the Chinese *Anti-Japan War Game* or anti-Israeli *Special Force*—or even pondering their premises—could experience a kind of cognitive dissonance, a confrontation with a very different worldview. By interacting with the blinkered viewpoint of another national ideology, the gamer could begin to see the cultural limits inherent in games made to cater to one's own cultural experience. As Galloway notes, the very existence of games like *Under Ash* and *Special Force* have the potential to reveal how peculiarly American are the viewpoints presented in games like *America's Army, Full Spectrum Warrior,* or *Conflict: Desert Storm.*

Still, one would hope for games that explore solutions less deadly than the us-versus-them mentality of the real-life conflicts they seek to emulate. One such attempt is a game developed in 2005 at Carnegie Mellon University, devoted to exploring possibilities for peace in Israeli-Palestinian relations. Called *PeaceMaker*, it is a single-player turn-based strategy game, like *SimCity* or *Civilization*, meant for educational use by "Israelis, Palestinians and young adults worldwide." The user takes on the role of either the Israeli prime minister or Palestinian president, and then manages scenarios based on real occurrences. According to the game's Web site, "the player must react to in-game events, from diplomatic negotiations to military attacks, and interact with eight other political leaders and social groups in order to establish a stable resolution to the conflict before his or her term in office ends." A high score merits a "Nobel Prize Winner" distinction; the lowest possible scorer is ranked as "War Criminal." Perhaps *PeaceMaker* will become the *Oregon Trail* of the Age of Terror.

Sideshow of Force

One need not explore as far afield as Chinese or Islamist gaming to experience ideological discord: an underground world of no-budget underground American games that cropped up during the tumultuous aftershocks of 9/11 and the War on Terror can provide just as potent a dose of culture shock. A decade ago, the advent of Macromedia Flash allowed for a whole new type of do-it-yourself, low-tech game that melded the simple play of old-school video games with *South Park*-style cartoon graphics. In the late 1990s, one popular kind of Flash games was the celebrity assassin genre: little shoot-'em-up created so the player can terminate the Spice Girls, Hanson, Eminem, or Jar Jar Binks. In these brief, gory gunfests, animated photos purloined from gossip magazines are defaced with rifle blasts, blood splotches, and chainsaw wounds.

Assassin games were the descendants of the old pop-sicko *Doom* mods, gone mainstream in a broadband era. Often structured like ultrashort first-person shooters, the assassin games don't have much game play to speak of, and are often open-ended free-for-alls or gaming equivalents of one-liners. Simply excuses for ridiculous acts of abuse, they satisfy an urge to deal symbolic harm by defacing someone's image, which is why so many employ photographs. Assassin games give the same basic satisfaction obtained by scribbling over the face of your nemesis in a high school yearbook.

When Newgrounds, a site that aggregates homemade Flash content, started compiling these celebrity shoot-outs, the makers of assassin games began to one-up each other with increased levels of gore, absurdity, juvenility, or even design sophistication. Though many contributors are effectively anonymous, most seem to be teenagers or college-aged. The archives on these sites now seem like kid-culture mini-museums, with games devoted to murdering Pokémon, the Spice Girls, Gap models, and, in one instance, "Steve, the faggot in denial" from *Blue's Clues*.

After 9/11, that magical date when everything changed, celebrity assassin games underwent a notable transformation as well, and the invisible army of Internet Flash artists quickly rolled out a new assassin subgenre. Within days of the attacks, when many Americans were still confused, anxiety-ridden, and pissed off, games appeared on the Internet that allowed you to shoot, kick, punch, electrocute, or nuke Osama Bin Laden, helping players point and click toward some modicum of catharsis. In one game, you can shave off his beard with an electric razor; in another, force the Al Qaeda leader to snort an enormous amount of cocaine. Free Osama "skins" began circulating for multiplayer games *Unreal Tournament* and *Quake3: Arena*, allowing players of these shootfests to transform a character into Bin Laden for the sole purpose of blasting him to hell over and over again. These anti-Osama games are the latter-day equivalents of the Gulf War's *Spit on Saddam*—interactive political cartoons, war totems, and digital voodoo dolls—but play to a more organic desire for retribution.

Newgrounds creator Tom Fulp wrote such classic celebrity assassin titles as *Beat up Backstreet Boys!* and *Britney Spears Truck Jump*. Just three days after 9/11, Fulp uploaded a game he had quickly designed called *Bad Dudes vs Bin Laden,* inspired by the 1988 street-fighting game *Bad Dudes vs Dragon Ninja*. In the sick-cute little death match, players control an old-school tough guy in long hair, muscle-tee, and high-tops, who throws some badass martial arts moves at Bin Laden until the Saudi terrorist leader's head flies off, as eight-bit pseudo-Arabic music loops in the background. Fulp acknowledged that there were real-life bad dudes who used 9/11 as an excuse for racist violence. As the game opens, the Bad Dudes announce that "We've got no problem with our Arab buddies . . . Except for one," and the game repeats this warning at its end, this time delivered by the Bad Dudes on the White House lawn with Ronald Reagan.

Fulp added a further explanation on Newgrounds. "I've been very conflicted ever since the attack on NYC," he wrote. "I was considering making a tribute movie that portrayed the positive acts that occurred during the aftermath, but eventually decided to stick with my roots and make a violent video game. I have a hard time trying new things. I wasn't sure if a game would be appropriate, but I realized that it really is. You see, America is very sad right now, but it is also very ANGRY. People need a way to vent their frustrations, and I feel this can help. I also tried to pack the game with a positive message. There are a lot of nice people in my city who wear turbans, and I don't want people giving them dirty looks just because of some wacko terrorists. So with that said, go kick Bin Laden's ass!" These Osama-whacking splatterfests may be goofy, but they take as their premise the need to react to an actual traumatic event, and thus tap into a kind of righteous hatred considerably less trivial than mere annoyance with boy bands or Britney. The games can be seen as cathartic for both makers and users: a taste of sweet revenge came both in the act of their creation and in play.

Another early game, Matt Chase's *Whack Osama*, refashions the arcade and fairground favorite Whac-A-Mole: photos of Bin Laden pop up out of holes so you can smash them with a mallet. *Blow Osama to Hell*, by Newgrounds user stuntmonkey666, sends a photo-montaged George W. Bush himself to kill Osama with a pistol. After firing rounds at his body (which collapses limb by limb, like a George Romero zombie), Bush holds Bin Laden's bloody, severed head in victory. Drugfilms' *Osamagotchi* provides more elaborate means of destroying Bin Laden. Its name is a play on the Japanese Tamagotchi, a "virtual pet" key-chain toy whose owner assumed responsibility for the simulated animal's care and feeding. In *Osamagotchi*, the user assumes responsibility for Bin Laden's torture. Under a cartoon of a shirtless Bin Laden in a desert, players choose a variety of violent options from a panel of buttons. Some are straightforward, like a gun that blasts dripping-red holes in his body, or a baseball bat that bitch-slaps his head from side to side. Others are parodic-patriotic. You can make a bald eagle attacks his head, stick American flags into his body, or order Ronald McDonald and Grimace to assault him. One button makes two anime-style nudie babes appear behind him, bare breasts bobbing —insulting his fundamentalist mores, perhaps, but otherwise causing no harm. *Osamagotchi* is bizarre enough that it's difficult to tell whether its violent jingoism is in earnest or ironic, though it's probably both.

Given these dark underpinnings, it's no surprise that some games verge into unsavory territory. In the crude first-person shooter *Bin Laden Liquors*, produced by Fieler Media in 2001 and found on various Web sites, Bin Laden is the proprietor of an American-style liquor store—"secret headquarters of the Al Qaeda," a title declares—in a reference to the Arab-American convenience-store owner cliché. "No attempt to stereotype, condemn or discriminate against any given race, religion, nationality or occupation (except terrorism) is either expressed or implied," a lame disavowal reads before the action begins. Fieler created the equally cynical *Mind the Bombs* right after the 2005 terrorist attacks in London; in it, players must laser-zap cartoon bombs as they pop up on a map of the London Underground. Neither one of these games appears on Newgrounds, and Fieler's original site for their Osama shooter has disappeared; *Bin Laden Liquors* lives on, however, traded and hosted on numerous home pages.

Fulp also created an Osama game with creepy overtones of prisoner torture, although it was uploaded prior to the Abu Ghraib revelations. A departure from the retro whimsy of *Bad Dudes vs. Bin Laden*, Fulp's 2002 *Al Qaidamon* joins in *Bin Laden Liquors'* vicious spirit. In another takeoff on the virtual pet fad (specifically Pokémon's Gameboy incarnation), the player has to "take care of" an orange-suited, bearded prisoner in a dungeonlike cell. If you give him doughnuts or brush his beard, a barometer rises from "Geneva Convention" to "Human Rights Activists Approved." Stop feeding him, or batter his face with a boxing glove, and his rating drops all the way down to "Hitler's Approval." At that point, the player can shoot the imprisoned terrorist to death with a gun. "This of course was inspired by the activists who feel we are too hard on our prisoners," Fulp explain in his description. "Now it is up to you to decide!"

A user with the screen name "ViolaVillainess" left this response to *Al Qaidamon* in 2005: "well . . . maybe it's my sick and twisted little mind . . . but i wanted more options . . . maybe u could have more places where u could shoot him . . . a knife would be nice . . . and what's the point of putting him in his underwear if u can't low blow him? I'd like for him to bleed more. I'd like for him to respond . . . maybe some yells and screams . . . to be suffering he doesn't express a lot of agony . . . why can't we stone him or drown him? since it's jus a game . . . go all out . . . but i still like it . . . but i'm an angry ANGRY person . . . with issues . . . and i need more VIOLENCE . . ."

Blood Lust

The ultimate anti-Bin Laden game went beyond the realm of Macromedia Flash, crafting an elaborate revenge fantasy in the form of a full-fledged first-person shooter adventure. Jason Huddy created *Blood of Bin Laden* from the engine for *Marathon*, a game from the mid-nineties for Mac by Bungie. *Blood of Bin Laden* has the logic of the other Bin Laden assassin games, but pushes the real-life revenge theme to even greater levels of bombastic excess and absurdity. The front page of the game's short-lived Web site (taken down in late 2003) looks like a John Heartfield agit-surrealist photomontage revisited for the Fox News age, cramming together a composition of Bin Laden's face, gas-masked desert soldiers, a map of Afghanistan, and a laptop displaying photos of the September 11th hijackers. Its navigation menu is built on a belt of machine-gun bullets. "*Blood of Bin Laden* is more than just a means of satisfying America's post 9/11 bloodlust," the site's "About B.O.B.L." section reads.

"It's a game that accurately re-creates the exciting events of Operation Enduring Freedom, allowing players to fight the War on Terrorism without leaving their desktop!"

The game begins in Afghanistan, right after the Al Qaeda-engineered suicide bombing of the USS *Cole* in 2000. The player assumes the role of an American covert operative on a mission to destroy those responsible for the bombing; in a terrorist training camp, he finds literal blueprints for the September 11 attacks. The action then shifts to Operation Enduring Freedom, during which the player fights Taliban in Kabul (and rescues American missionary Heather Mercer), and ends with a raid on Bin Laden's palatial underground hideaway beneath the caves of Tora Bora. The finale is the chance to kill Bin Laden himself, who is armed with a shoulder-mounted rocket launcher. The game also has an "Instant Gratification Level," which allows players to jump right to the final scene, and kill an army of Bin Laden clones over and over again.

In a parody of big-budget military games' stated obsession with realism, *Blood of Bin Laden* carries over its photomontage aesthetic into the game itself. Almost everything in the low-res game environment has been converted from newswire photos: Afghan huts, destroyed architecture, U.S. convoys, bright yellow food packets, and nearly identical bright yellow cluster bombs. Enemies are designed from photos of Huddy and his friends dressed up in cheap costumes as suicide bombers, Taliban war-riors, and Al Qaeda gunmen, bumped down to chunky-pixeled characters. Some of the most spectacular visuals in the game are the screens that open each chapter, also collaged from photos into a superglossed, heightened reality, satirizing news channel graphic bombastics. The USS *Cole* blossoms an impossibly beautiful plume of smoke, Taliban crouch in snowy mountain crags, and jetliners zoom ahistorically toward the Twin Towers in unison, which appears backlit by a golden rising sun, while throngs of New Yorkers flood the Brooklyn Bridge below, as in a biblical epic. The final screen is one of Saddam Hussein, looking out over a golden desert emblazoned with the question "Next time . . . IRAQ?"

Before *Blood of Bin Laden*, Huddy created another *Marathon* variant called *Los Disneys* in 1998. Set in a future world in which Florida had been taken over by the Disney corporation, the game had players shooting their way through the Magic Kingdom, slaughtering trademarked characters and Michael Eisner clones amid the screams of tourist children. "Americans are angry," Huddy told a *Wired* reporter in a story about the game. "They come home, and they want to kill the boss. Instead of climbing a bell tower with a sniper rifle, they can play *Los Disneys*."

Americans may have still been angry in 2002, but their focus had shifted or expanded from corporations to terrorists. Our world had been handed a new map on which to chart our hatreds and anxieties. "We hope our game serves not only as a means of satisfying American gamers' post 9-11 thirst for vengeance," Huddy concludes on the *Blood of Bin Laden* site, "but also, and more importantly, as a first-hand history lesson to the few who didn't have their eyes glued to the television set every waking moment of that truly historic period. And remember . . . If you don't play our game, the terrorists have already won."

Go USA

By pushing their violent, absurd humor to the extreme, games like *Osamagotchi* and *Blood of Bin Laden* convey an ambiguous political valence. They can be taken as examples of American patriotism gone wild, or overblown parodies of the same. *Al Qaidamon* probably falls just inside the border of in the former camp, while *Blood of Bin Laden* is definitely closer to the latter. Like games in general, the meaning of the actions performed involves the subjective experience of the player. In this regard, ViolaVillaness's creepy Livejournal-style response to *Al Qaidamon* feels particularly disturbing, since she seems to impart no greater meaning to a game based on prisoner torture at all: her desire to see more detailed elements of torture because she is "ANGRY" reads less like an opinion and more like an underexamined cultural symptom. (Then again, as is often the case with Internet postings, maybe she's just some kid talking shit.)

Indeed, at a certain level, many would consider it a quixotic gesture to read too much moral meaning into a genre that is expressly designed to explore the limits of bad taste: after all, some the earliest games on Newgrounds were devoted to clubbing baby seals. If these games were just about sending Bad

Dudes to kick Osama's butt, they could be seen as a harmless, populist responses to a traumatic event. But months after 9/11, Newgrounds' archive of assassin games contained substantial subsections devoted not just to games about mutilating Bin Laden, but Saddam Hussein and Kim Il Jong II as well. These bluntly political games parallel the Bush administration's own transference of enemy status from Bin Laden to the Axis of Evil—even if specifically anti-Iran games have yet to surface, no doubt due to the lack of an Baruch Goldstein–style figurehead to punch, kick, or spit on. Like ViolaVillainess, many of us may indeed enjoy dealing out virtual violence in games: one of the great joys of the Internet is exploring forbidden desires without real-life repercussions. Yet here lies a trove of evidence pointing to how effectively we can be influenced by a leader with an agenda as to where we should direct our anger. For all the rebellious in-your-faceness of the Newgrounds aesthetic, so much of the user-submitted content appears to be uncritically compliant with the desires of the Bush administration.

This is demonstrated to the fullest extent in Newgrounds 2002 entry *TerrorWar–Da PAYBACK* by EvilDave, in which the player points-and-clicks nuclear strikes on a map of the Middle East, guided by red stars indicating sites like Palestine, Afghanistan, Iran, Mecca, Baghdad, "Qatar, Home of Al-Jazeera the Raghead Network," and, for bonus amusement, France. Responses to *TerrorWar* remain archived on the site. "Next to banging some supermodel, im sure this is everyone's fantasy, nuking the shit out of the middle east. GREAT FUCKING GAME!" wrote Purebastard a few days after the game's release. "FUCK MECCA!!! THOSE RAGHEAD CAMEL FUCKING TERROR-ISTS FLEW A COUPLE OF PLANES INTO THE WORLD TRADE CENTER, KILLING THOUSANDS OF PEOPLE, SO WHY SHOULDN'T WE BOMB THE FUCK OUT OF MECCA???" screamed another user in a post entitled "GAME DOESN'T GO FAR ENOUGH!!!!" while others added, "A good game to vent out your anger regarding Sept11! GO USA, KICK SOME ASS!" and "Woohoo! I got israel! Die Jew Die!!!!!" (A small minority of responses criticized the game; "someone ought to blow you up, you racist fuck," wrote one user.)

Repugnant responses like those quoted above are reminders of the possibility for games to be used to reinforce hatred. Like cinema, literature, or other forms of media, games are certainly not immune from this potential, and they add the ability for players to perform symbolic actions of violence against repre-sentations of their particular enemies. This is why game pub-lishers often create politically correct good-guy characters in war-themed games, as if to defuse this aspect: *Viet-Cong* has South Vietnamese nonplayer characters as part of your squad, *Medal of Honor: Rising Sun* includes a Japanese-American spy who helps the Marines infiltrate Tokyo, the commercial version of *Full Spectrum Warrior* includes an Arab-American soldier in one squad, and *America's Army* offers the option of playing dis-concertingly ambiguous "indigenous forces," who are identified as a "unique class [that] mimics the real life indigenous allied forces that work with U.S. Special Forces around the globe," according to the game's site. The over-the-top ultraviolent arcade game *Target: Terror* includes scenarios that mimic contemporary events and fears (in one sequence, players must kill hijackers of an airliner who intend to crash it into the White House), but the terrorists are depicted as not specifically Middle Eastern but rather, in the words of its developer, "ethnically ambiguous."

With games created outside mainstream commercial channels, however, open hatred can be unleashed freely, without fear of reprisal from government censorship panels or poor sales. There is something of a minor tradition in virulently racist white power games, for instance. Resistance Records, the official music label of the American neo-Nazi organization National Alliance, distributes a game called *Ethnic Cleansing*, in which the player moves through a virtual New York City in order to slaughter blacks, Latinos, and Jews. The player can outfit his protagonist as a contemporary skinhead, or in more retro Ku Klux Klan hood and robe. Earlier versions of the same idea include the German game *Concentration Camp Manager*, a crude simulation that awards points for killing Jews and Turks, Nazi mods for *Doom* (such as *Nazi Doom* and *WP Doom*), a Pac-Man takeoff called *SA Mann*, *Concentration Camp Rat Hunt*, which involves shooting Jews inside the Auschwitz death camp, and something simply called *Shoot the Blacks*.

There are a handful of Newgrounds games that allow play from outside the American perspective. *Kaboom! The Suicide Bomber Game* is drawn like a children's book: you play a suicide bomber and win points by killing people on a street. Needless to say, it is a one-round game. But even here the game is framed with its author's supposedly apolitical stance (according to his profile, he was seventeen when he wrote it): "By the way, I'm not jewish, I'm not an arab, and I'm not a terrorist. I have little interest in what goes on in the middle east so I don't share any extreme views. I just think people who blow themselves up are stupid. That's all this game is. If anything this is going to be an anti-Yasser Arafat game . . . If you found this offensive, tell your friends! If you are DEEPLY offended by this game then you're way too fucking sensitive for my taste and I hope that you've been scarred for life." (Despite the author's stated intention, *Kaboom!* also appears on neo-Nazi Web sites, who contextualize it as an opportunity to kill Jews.) More bizarre is *Fly into the World Trade Center*, a primitive flight simulator that zooms over a cityscape filled with endless replicas of the Twin Towers, which the player is meant to smash into over and over again. The humor here is not specifically anti-American, but plays with the shock of the forbidden.

Thinking back to Galloway's analysis of Arab games versus *America's Army*, it's instructive to compare the jingo-nihilistic batch of Newgrounds games with those of French Web site Uzinagaz, which likewise traffic in clever flash pastimes with naughty content, but do so from a slightly different worldview.

For example, Uzinagaz's celebrity assassin game is the medievalish *Axe Throw* (or *Lance La Hache*), in which famous figures are spread-eagled on a wooden plank as targets for a series of hatchets. Players can choose from a wide variety of political personalities, including George W. Bush, Condoleezza Rice, Tony Blair, Jacques Chirac, Jean Chretien, "Oussama Ben Laden," Saddam Hussein, Slobodan Milosovic, "Muqtada Al-Sadr," and Fidel Castro. As of late 2005, Bush hit number one on Axe Throw's "Kill Parade" of "most killed top listing," while Chirac is listed at number three.

Possibly the most well-known Uzinagaz game, however is a 9/11-themed number called *New York Defender*, created by a duo by the name of Stef and Phil. According to Uzinagaz, the game has been played more than a million and a half times (the most popular Newgrounds games also claim to have been viewed over one million times). *New York Defender* has a similar logic to eighties arcade game *Missile Command*: you control a powerful laser cannon to destroy a nonstop series of hijacked airliners tearing through a clear blue sky toward the World Trade Center. If a plane crashes successfully, it leaves a smoking scar. If more than one plane hits, the towers crumble in on themselves in a plume of gray smoke. Though at first the planes are easy to zap, soon there are so many that saving the Towers is ultimately impossible. The games' directions simply state (in English): "Use your mouse to fight the feeling of impotence," but this is ironic: it is a game that cannot be won. Thus *New York Defender* could be seen as a statement on the futility of fighting terrorism, or the irreversibility of historical events. September 11 happened; it cannot be undone, even through the fantasy of a game.

Uzinagaz's *Baghdad Defender* is almost identical in game play to *New York Defender*, but looks onto the nighttime skies over the Iraqi city, where the player must zap incoming missiles. When hit, Baghdad glows a deep orange. The game does not state whose perspective is portrayed: Saddam Hussein's army? Insurgents? Heavily armed peace activists? Or perhaps, like *New York Defender*, you play a purely philosophical construct: the desire for events to have been otherwise. In any case, the mirror-image parallels between *New York Defender* and *Baghdad Defender* are themselves meaningful. From the point of view of the city dweller, the attacks are equated; like *New York Defender*, the *Baghdad Defender* player is told to use his or her mouse "to fight the feeling of impotence." This, it seems, is the real battle being depicted in the games, and their meaning is deepened in relation to one another.

The French site also includes a game based on the war in Afghanistan, called *Enduring Freedom*. In it, you fly a bomber over a vertically scrolling desert landscape, dotted with villages, oases, tanks, and terrorist training camps. It's not too dissimilar to eighties games like Activision's *River Run*, except instead of blocky eight-bit graphics, the icons representing civilian and military areas are round and cartoon-bubbly. The object is to bomb the bad guys without bombing civilian villages. It's not a hard game, but with every wrong move, you cannot help but feel a slight tinge of remorse; after all, you've just killed some innocent people—maybe a wedding party. "Game Over: you have murdered too many peaceful civilians," the game sternly announces at the end of one round, yet might add simultaneously, "Congratulations! You enter top ten scores!"

Antiwar Games

While the Newgrounds' teens were busy crafting novel ways to torture virtual terrorists, other flash designers promulgated games that took a more direct antiwar stance than those of Uzinagaz. One of the earliest to emerge was New Zealander Josh On's *Antiwargame,* a cunningly designed mini-war simulation with an overtly leftist tack. On is best known for a later 2002 Web work, *They Rule,* which allows users to map the personal connections among members of presidential cabinets, boards of directors of major corporations, and other elite institutions—almost like a Friendster for the ruling class. *Antiwargame* likewise deploys a Chomskyesque politics, but more in the allegorical manner of a political cartoon than a visualized database.

The player takes the role of an American president (Uncle Sam or Aunt Samantha), who must made decisions in the wake of a major terrorist attack. The game consists of two landscapes, each populated by small mushroomlike people—a map of the United States, and a desert dotted with a few oil wells—as well as a manipulatable pie chart indicating budget levels for Military/ Business, Social Spending, and Foreign Aid. The little Americans appear as either blue civilians or green military. Using pull-down menus on each citizen, the player can send soldiers to the desert to annex oil wells or draft them into the National Guard to quell war protesters. Once the oil-guarding soldiers start killing desert dwellers, "media" with cameras appear, who can be chased away using military officers. Throughout the course of the war, the player must balance the budget in response to events as they occur. When a terrorist threat is announced, for example, the game suggests increasing Foreign Aid. If the Military/Business wedge becomes too narrow, a business leader has the president "assassinated" and the game ends.

Achieving an optimal budget in the course of *Antiwargame* is difficult and may be impossible. The only way to avoid disastrous events appears to be to choose to do nothing: do not alter the budget significantly and do not send troops to the desert. The political message of *Antiwargame* is determined primarily by the structure of its game play—yoking Military and Business spending into one category, for example, or dictating that increased Foreign Aid will quell terrorists in ways that military actions will not. Thus the message of *Antiwargame* is as reductive, in its own way, as *America's Army*. *Antiwargame* creates its own miniature fantasy world that does not, for example, allow for the idea that terrorism could ever merit a legitimate military response. In *Antiwargame*, war happens merely to secure oil wells, and results in increased domestic terrorism—a notion that the invasion of Afghanistan and ongoing military efforts to disrupt the Al Qaeda network would seem to counter, even if the invasion of Iraq does not. An important distinction, however, is that *Antiwargame* openly announces itself as a political allegory—a parody, even—while Army-subsidized games like *America's Army* or *Full Spectrum Warrior* do not. Like a political cartoon, *Antiwargame* presents an openly partisan argument or point of view, rather than pretending to aspire to mimetic realism.

A similar comparison could be made between *Kuma\War* and Newsgaming.com, an Uruguay-based project spearheaded by Gonzalo Frasca, a designer who has also written extensively on theoretical aspects of video gaming, and a "team of independent game developers who believe video games are not simply an amusement." Like *Kuma\War*, Newsgaming states that its goal is to produce games that respond to current events as they occur. But instead of games steeped in tactical simulations of real-life melees, Newsgaming offers, in its own words, "simulation meets political cartoons" that "can also make us think about what is going on in this world."

Newsgaming uploaded *September 12th, a toy world* to its site in 2003. In this piece, the player must attempt to kill black-robed, gun-toting terrorists as they skulk through the narrow pathways of a cutely cartooned Middle Eastern town, making sure not to kill the blue-robed civilian adults and children they move among. But the player's missiles prove to be unreliably messy: it is impossible to strike the terrorists without destroying nearby buildings and civilians. When each civilian dies, the body remains on the ground near the cartoon rubble, and other tiny civilian figures appear next to it, weeping audibly; before long, the mourners transform into terrorists themselves. The game has no end and, again, cannot be won: after a few rounds of missiles, the town is overrun by terrorists. *September 12th* achieves a similar effect to *New York Defender* or *Baghdad Defender*, but is more explicit in proposing an intended antiwar message of violence begetting violence.

Kabul Kaboom! is another game created by Frasca, prior to the Newsgaming project, with a blunter urgency. On his Web site, Frasca explains that the game was created very quickly, during a single airplane trip in 2001. "I was on a United flight with my wife on [September 11], and the next time that I had to fly I decided to create a game as a way to deal with my fear," Frasca writes, paralleling many of the statements of Newgrounds game designers, many of whom likewise claim that their games were designed as a means to confront their own post-9/11 emotions . "By that time, there were many anti-Osama online games but, as much as I dislike Osama, I decided to focus on another event . . . I was disgusted at seeing how the most powerful country on earth was bombing the crap out of one of the poorest." Frasca designed *Kabul Kaboom!* as a takeoff on the eighties bomb-catching game *Kaboom!*. In Frasca's "humanitarian game for a 'humanitarian' war," players try to catch hamburgers falling from the sky without getting struck by missiles that rain down with them. The player's character is an image lifted from Picasso's *Guernica* of a woman wailing to the heavens as she cradles a dead baby. One quickly discovers the game is almost impossible to play, and it ends abruptly; the final screen is a photo of a bombed-out building strewn with more *Guernica* body parts and a restart button marked "GAME NOT OVER–PLAY AGAIN."

The most humorous of the antiwar game crop is not really a game at all, but rather a click-through flash sideshow imitating turn-based strategy games like *Civilization*. Dermot O'Connor posted his *Gulf War 2 (aka World War 2.5)* in late 2002. The "player" takes the role of a dumbfounded President Bush, who is guided by his advisers to enter a war in Iraq that escalates into an all-out Middle East nuclear conflict, which transpires on a map of the region dotted with icons for armies, missiles, stealth bombers, and other forces. Cheney, Powell, Rumsfeld, Rice, and Ashcroft all appear as taking-head icons, in the manner of the advisers in *Civilization*, and wartime events pop up with messages spoofing those in Sid Meyer's game. "Baghdad crater is liberated!" announces one such update after U.S. forces finish bombing the capital. Despite its lighthearted tone, O'Connor's game received a great deal of hate mail, ten pages of which he has posted to his site. "You must be French. I think your web site sucks. Why don't you move to Iraq? Communist hippy," reads one (O'Connor is in fact Irish). "Quite possibly the stupidest thing I've ever seen! I guess we need to have another September 11th before people like you wake up and realize who we are dealing with here. Maybe you should go live over in Iraq for a while and then you can come home and thank your lucky stars that you are an AMERICAN! (you are an American, aren't you?)" another suggests.

Not all antiwar games took the structure of shooter games as their basis, however. Urtica, an artists' group based in Belgrade, Serbia, created an online game called *Lapsus Memoriae* in 2002. Players click on gray squares arranged in a grid of four by five, briefly revealing pairs of black and white icons that resemble corporate logos. The goal, as in the card game Concentration, is to match pairs of symbols. When the player makes a match, the screen shifts to an animated display of the icon, which is revealed to literalize the official names of military actions from the War on Terror or the post-Communist wars in the Balkans, ranging from Operation Infinite Justice (the temporary name for the 2001 war on Afghanistan) to Operation Amber Fox (a contemporary NATO action in Macedonia, symbolized by a stylized fox's tail). According to its designers, *Lapsus Memoriae* is about the way such brandlike names evoke "an unconscious erasure of all negative connotations connected to the concept they refer to." Its makers may or may not also realize that it recalls card games used in the nineteenth century to train French officers in military terms, World War II card decks that taught American soldiers to identify the shapes of

Japanese and German aircraft, or even the famous "Most Wanted Iraqis" playing cards developed by the U.S. Military in Iraq. *Lapsus Memoriae* ends when all the pairs have been matched, but in their statement about the game, Urtica says that "in this game nobody wins."

Most of the antiwar games mentioned—*New York Defender*, *Baghdad Defender*, *Antiwargame*, *Kabul Kaboom!*, and *September 12th*—all share a similar trait: they are games that cannot be won. (Even Newgrounds features one anti-war game from 2002 along these lines, *Enduring Pipeline*, which is similar in structure to *September 12th*, but enacted with mere stick figures.) A hackneyed sentiment about war-as-a-game, perhaps, but in the context of video games, it is one that can be made on an experiential level rather than simply that of content. Gonzalo Frasca argues that video games have traditionally limited their outcomes to a mere "binary" win/lose structure. The outcomes of real war, of course, are far more complicated than this, but most commercial war video games avoid this fact by focusing on the acts of single individuals or small groups of characters. Thus the Vietnam War cannot be won by American troops in *Viet-Cong: Purple Haze*, nor does the Intifada overthrow the Israeli government in *Under Ash*, but in both cases the survival of the protagonist becomes the game's goal. By throwing out the option of winning, antiwar games refuse to allow for even this limited feeling of triumphalism.

Anne Frank as Princess Toadstool

At the same time, a more nuanced exploration of war is possible in games, beyond a simple—and simplistic—structure predicated on either the experience of victory or its denial.

In his essay "Ephemeral Games: Is it barbaric to design video games after Auschwitz?," Frasca describes a hypothetical version a game that could take on a topic as serious as the Holocaust. (Frasca's essay takes its title from a famous phrase by philosopher Theodor Adorno, who stated that it would be barbaric to write lyric poetry after Auschwitz: an event of world-historical ghastliness should never be aestheticized.) Regardless of content, using a normal video game to portray the Holocaust would be offensive, Frasca argues, for reasons inherent in the very structure of video games as we know them. Because the game can be restarted, the player would not feel the weight of moral responsibility. "For example," Frasca writes, a player "would be able to betray other prisoners and make the guards shoot them. In case the rest of the prisoners would react by criticizing or even attacking him, all he would need to do is to restore a previously saved version and he would be able to get away with his crimes. In other words, the environment could become a simulator for sadists"—not unlike actual racist games that appear on neo-Nazi sites.

This observation can be easily extended to military video games. In *Conflict: Desert Storm*, for example, the player can pick off civilian Iraqi farmers and shepherds if he or she wishes,

or even play target practice on goats. Whether this constitutes true sadism is debatable, but it undoubtedly happens without the "weight of moral responsibility" that such real-world actions would merit. But often designers seem to take this sadism-simulator potential into account. In many games, it is impossible to shoot your compatriots, or even anybody aside from designated enemies: unloading ammo into them has no effect at all. In *America's Army*, soldiers are removed from the game for a period of time if they let off friendly fire. In neither case are these actions given the dramatic or tragic import they would in, say, a film or graphic novel.

More perniciously, Frasca postulates, the very nature of a typical video game's win-lose logic would make the Holocaust "a secondary issue, an object to overcome." This is not dissimilar to Clive Thompson's claim that Japanese gamers saw little import in the content of the Pearl Harbor-themed *Medal of Honor: Rising Sun*; after all, most war games play out in more or less similar fashions, with only superficial differences in styles of weaponry, type of terrain, and ethnicity of opponents. "If we followed that logic," Frasca says, "the player could follow a 'correct' path in order to save Anne Frank from death," and with the ability to restart a failed mission, life and death "would lose their ethical, historical and social value." By extension, one could say that any ethical qualms or historical resonances felt by the player—such as my déjà vu in playing *Rising Sun*—would be determined outside the game itself, and thus beyond the control of the designer. A neo-Nazi, for example, might use Frasca's Holocaust game as a means to delight in Anne Frank's slaughter.

A contemporary equivalent of Frasca's Holocaust game could be a game in which you play someone trapped in the Twin Towers during the September 11th attacks. In fact, a notorious proposal for such a game did surface in 2003. Called *9-11 Survivor*, it never got beyond a few examples of concept art posted to its Web site, which were enough to cause outrage on their own. Frasca criticized *9-11 Survivor*'s premise on his blog, Ludology.org, calling it "nothing but the Disneylandation of terror," spurring a great deal of blogger discussion.

In order to avoid these dangers, Frasca suggests a hypothetical video game with a highly experimental structure. Such a game would be single-player, so as to allow the designer more control over its play. Its narrative should be irreversible, so the player would have to deal with the consequences of his or her actions without being able to simply restart; by extension, when game characters died, their demise would be realistically irrevocable. Most radically, any given player should only be allowed to play a given game a single time, in order to ensure its irreversibility and finality. For this final requirement, Frasca suggests that his hypothetical games could be "scheduled," as unique events. "Our only solution would be to transform the game into a happening"–borrowing terminology from the one-off countercultural art events of the 1960s. "The game could be scheduled for, let's say, next Monday at 8 P.M. Every player would have to log in at that moment to start playing. After that, nobody else would be able to start playing that game, ever. It would be the exact equivalent of missing a happening: you simply can not show up three days later."

Frasca's hypothetical Holocaust game remains a philosophical toy rather than a real one, but is nonetheless interesting to ponder as a kind of mythical object. It should be considered not so much an actual blueprint, but a commentary on how far outside the norm designers might have to go to make video games about real war that approach the gravity and nuance of older art forms like literature or painting—games that work not just as entertainment, but as art. In this example, Frasca suggests that games might have to become a little less like games as we have come to know them, and a bit more like theater.

The Art of War

The concept of video games as art is nonetheless a fait accompli: during the same first five years of the new millennium in which real war became an important new theme for commercial games, a new generation of visual artists began to use game technologies in their work. By 2005, the practice had gone from underground to trendy. And many of the best of these game artists have at one time or another taken on the topic of war—an unsurprising confluence, given the frequency of that same theme in commercial games. Noncommercial games like *Los*

Disneys, September 12th, Lapsus Memoriae, and *They Rule* have all been classified as art upon occasion, as museums, curators, biennials, and galleries have extended their reach onto the Internet. One might even consider the anti-Osama games as a form of digital folk art. Like more traditional artworks, these games have either a single author or a relatively small group of authors as opposed to a corporate imprimatur; they are intended to convey a message, meaning, or experience not otherwise available through commercial entertainment; sometimes they are virtuoso expressions of programming cleverness or design wit—a legacy of the hacker culture of the 1960s. Like commercial games, game artworks can succeed or not, but their goals and standards of value are very different. Most importantly, the line between high art and homemade fun is not always clear, however—Huddy's *Blood of Bin Laden* could be taken as a work of ironic art that purloins mass-media culture in the pop traditions of Warhol or Rauschenberg, or it could thought of as just some fucked-up thing someone made because it was sick-cool. In a field so new, the distinctions among commercial designer, amateur hacker, and studio artist are frequently irrelevant.

The fact that many of these games do not seem to allow for a salable object in the manner of paintings or sculpture does not hinder this classification, of course: the dematerialization of the art object is an old story by now, and contemporary art is well acquainted with such unmarketable art-stuff as performance art, Web-based art, conceptual art, and activist art. (And all have found a way to be bought and sold, in due time.)

Not all works of art made from games remain participatory; some artists have used game engines and footage from games to create works that are installed in a space as nonplayable video art pieces. A spectacular example is *Diplomatic Arena*, created in 2003 by Belgian-Canadian-American art-and-architecture collective Workspace Unlimited, using the engine for *Quake III Arena*. The artists populated vast gravity-free spaces with scores of armed, automated characters outfitted with the faces of terrorists and world leaders, programmed to frag one another endlessly in an orgy of carnage, forever blossoming with clouds of red blood and body parts. The sound track is an audio cut-up of CBS News—a copyright-infringing mash-up called "Rocked by Rape," by Evolution Control Committee—consisting of ominous headlines uttered by Dan Rather and driven by sampled AC/DC guitar riffs: "mysterious murder—chemical terrorism—military targets" and so on, in a looping litany of disaster. The upper left-hand corner of the screen keeps an ongoing tally of who's killed whom before they respawn and start all over again: "John Ashcroft ate Subcommandante Marcos's grenade," "Condoleezza Rice was shredded by Dick Cheney's shrapnel," "Al Gore Jr. was gunned down by Osama Bin Laden." The viewer can alter the point of view or perspective of the game as it plays itself, but that's all.

Workhouse borrows the slaughterhouse aesthetic of *Diplomatic Arena* from video games like *Quake* or the celebrity

assassin genre to create an object of contemplation. Adding
real-world figures into the gunfest brings any number of potential allegorical meanings to mind: one could interpret the work
as a commentary on how we must watch helplessly while these
figures wage eternal war with one another, and moreover do so
as a sort of entertainment. The work could be seen as a wish fulfillment: like twenty-first-century versions of the *Shahnama*'s
Kaid, world leaders have decided to stop deploying armies and
minions, and simply kill each other directly, leaving soldiers
and innocent civilians out of it. Certainly if, as in *Diplomatic
Arena*, Osama Bin Laden and George W. Bush had just shot at
one another and left it at that, our world would be a safer place.
Or perhaps *Diplomatic Arena* is simply a vision of Hell, where
power-hungry world leaders have been condemned to destroy
each other forever.

While not lifted directly from a video game, John Klima's 1999
Serbian Skylight might be the oldest artwork to deploy the visuals
of war-themed games. Installed horizontally, so the viewer looks
up into a video projection as if it is a window onto the sky, *Serbian
Skylight* displays CGI missiles falling downward. The number of
bombs is based on figures the Brooklyn-based Klima nicked from
Department of Defense briefings at the time regarding the American bombing of Kosovo that year, so *Serbian Skylight* serves as a
dramatic example of data visualization.

Klima pursued the same concept more elaborately in *The
Great Game*, a work from 2001, named after the term used

during the British Empire to describe that superpower's military and espionage operations in Afghanistan. Klima produced *The Great Game* at a time when images of the U.S. military action in Afghanistan were hard to come by; each day, like a news junkie, he sifted through the Department of Defense's written public reports online about the operation, and then rendered this information onto a digital, geologically contoured map of Afghanistan, using custom-made 3-D icons to represent aircraft, cities, military bases, humanitarian relief drop points, and other items. With several weeks of this data, he combined the maps into a Web-based Java applet that allows the user to zoom through the changing landscape via click-and-drag. It's as if Klima reconstituted a homemade analog of the same military simulations that one assumes American commanders used in the action event itself. Like *Diplomatic Arena, The Great Game* creates the sensation of a game we are allowed to watch, but not control; in this case, the model is a strategy game rather than a first-person shooter. Klima accentuated this aspect further when he moved *The Great Game* from the Internet to the gallery. As an installation, *The Great Game* runs on a video screen mounted to the front of a kiddie-sized blue helicopter ride (resembling, perhaps accidentally, the early Link "Blue Box" trainers). After the viewer sits inside the cockpit, the ride moves about on its own while the screen's image flies over an approximation of real wartime landscape.

A different kind of visualization is provided by British artists